9780935908329

Diagnosing and Treating
CO-DEPENDENCE

Diagnosing and Treating
CO-DEPENDENCE

A guide for
professionals who
work with chemical
dependents,
their spouses
and children

Timmen L. Cermak, M.D.

Johnson Institute Books
Professional Series
Minneapolis 1986

Copyright © 1986 by the Johnson Institute.
All rights reserved. No part of this book may be
reproduced or transmitted in any form or by any means,
electronic or mechanical, including photocopying,
recording, or by any information storage and retrieval
system without express permission in writing from the
publisher.

Published by Johnson Institute Books, 510 First Avenue
North, Minneapolis, Minnesota 55403.

Edited by Pamela Espeland.

Library of Congress Cataloging in Publication Data

Cermak, Timmen L.
  Diagnosing and treating co-dependence.

  Includes bibliographies and index.
  1. Substance abuse—Patients—Family relationships.
2. Family—Mental health. I. Title. [DNLM: 1. Family.
2. Substance Dependence—diagnosis. 3. Substance
Dependence—therapy. WM 270 C415d]
RC564.C45 1986   616.86   86-16119
ISBN: 0-935908-32-3

PRINTED IN THE UNITED STATES OF AMERICA

10 9 8 7 6 5 4 3

ACKNOWLEDGMENTS

Foremost is Stephanie Brown, Ph.D., whose vision helped open my eyes. I also wish to acknowledge my friends and colleagues on the Board of the National Association for Children of Alcoholics (NACoA). They have supported and challenged me as only a healthy family can.

Finally, I want to thank Carole Remboldt and the Johnson Institute for recognizing the need to advance the debate about co-dependence. Their support, and the editorial help of Pamela Espeland, have helped clarify my thinking throughout this book.

CONTENTS

Preface vii

Introduction: A New Look at Narcissus and Echo ix

PART ONE: DEFINING CO-DEPENDENCE 1
Levels of Meaning 2
Competing Theoretical Frameworks 4

PART TWO: DIAGNOSING CO-DEPENDENCE 9
Diagnostic Criteria for Co-Dependent Personality
  Disorder 11
Co-Dependent Variants 36
Clinical Examples and Transgenerational Diagrams 40
"Co-ing" vs. Helping 50
Special Concerns with Children and Adult Children
  of Alcoholics 54

PART THREE: TREATING CO-DEPENDENCE 61
General Considerations 62
The Stages of Recovery 68
Treatment for the Survival Stage (Stage I) 77
Treatment for the Re-identification Stage (Stage II) 81
Treatment for the Core Issues Stage (Stage III) 84
Treatment for the Re-integration Stage (Stage IV) 90
The Co-Dependent Professional 93

PART FOUR: THE FUTURE OF
  CO-DEPENDENCE 99

Afterword 105

Index 107

PREFACE

Co-dependence is both a legitimate psychological concept and an important human disorder. It represents a fascinating effort to understand a type of dysfunctional human behavior which is disturbingly prevalent. Therapists and other helping professionals in the chemical dependence (CD) field have found it to be a valuable framework for evaluating and treating the family dysfunction surrounding many chemically dependent clients.

Yet co-dependence has not gained total acceptance within the CD field, nor has it provoked much interest within the rest of the mental health community. Why? Because there has been no generally accepted definition of it. To date, most descriptions of co-dependence have been anecdotal or metaphoric, and neither anecdote nor metaphor stands up well under scientific scrutiny. It is time to define co-dependence at a level of sophistication at least equal to standards set forth in the *Diagnostic and Statistical Manual,* Third Edition (DSM III). Once we establish scientific validity and reliability for the concept, more professionals will take it seriously and we can advance our understanding of this major source of distress.

A definitive work on co-dependence is not yet possible. What *is* possible at this point is to develop a more complete framework for understanding co-dependence than has been available so far — one which is designed to interface directly with accepted psychiatric/psychologic concepts, language, and diagnostic systems. That is the goal of this book. I hope that this in turn will stimulate more effective and fruitful dialogue about co-dependence among members of the CD field and the mental health field at large, to the ultimate benefit of all families caught in the trap of chemical dependence.

The concept of co-dependence outlined herein assumes that chemical dependence is at least a fourfold disease. We are accustomed to thinking of it as having three facets — physical, emotional/psychological, and spiritual — all of which apply directly to the chemically dependent person himself or herself. But chemical dependence is also a *family* disease in the most profound sense of the word. Sooner or later, everyone around the sick person "catches" it in one form or another. And the primary vector in its transmission, both genetically and psychodynamically, is not restricted to the chemically dependent person alone. Rather, the disease passes through the family as a whole.

We must build the family aspect directly into our basic definition of the disease because it speaks so directly to the problem of prevention, as well as to treatment. Sad but true, we cannot in our lifetime treat each individual among the millions who already suffer from chemical dependence. Given the proper tools, however, we can go a long way toward ensuring that each succeeding generation suffers progressively less.

Timmen Cermak
1986

INTRODUCTION

A NEW LOOK AT NARCISSUS AND ECHO

The classic case of co-dependence was first presented by a Greek poet nearly 2,000 years ago. We know it as the tale of Narcissus and Echo from Ovid's *Metamorphoses*. Ovid didn't call Echo a co-dependent, but that is clearly what she was.

Echo was the fairest of the wood nymphs and quite a talker. That latter quality got her into trouble with Hera, wife of Zeus, king of the gods. When Hera suspected that Zeus was in love with one of the nymphs and set out to discover which, Echo distracted her with amusing chatter while the other nymphs stole away. Frustrated and angry, Hera turned against Echo. The goddess condemned her always to have the last word — but robbed her of the ability to initiate conversation. She would never again be able to speak except to repeat what was said to her.

This speech impediment was hardest to bear when Echo, like all the maidens before her, fell in love with Narcissus, a young man of great beauty. It is a misconception that Narcissus' fatal flaw lay in becoming enamored of his own reflection; this was actually a punishment visited on him by Nemesis, the goddess of righteous anger. Although everyone loved Narcissus, he refused to love anyone in return. He scorned those who adored him; their heartbreak meant nothing to him. Nemesis decided that if

Narcissus would not love others, he should be made to suffer a similar fate. And so it was that he was caused to fall in love with his own reflection.

Echo had no way to tell Narcissus how she felt about him. All she could do was follow him about, hoping for a scrap of attention. Her big chance came one day when Narcissus called out to his companions, "Is anyone here?" Echo was thrilled but too shy to meet him face-to-face. Instead, she remained hidden behind a tree and called back, "Here...here!" Narcissus looked around but saw no one. "Come!" he shouted. That was what Echo had been waiting for. Stepping forward, she beckoned to Narcissus and said sweetly, "Come."

But Narcissus turned away from her outstretched arms in disgust. "I will die before I give you power over me," he declared. To which Echo responded forlornly, "I give you power over *me*."

After Narcissus had left, Echo felt deeply ashamed. She crept into a cave and could not be comforted. Gradually she pined away with longing, her bones turning to stone and only her voice living on. Yet she continued to love Narcissus. Then came the day when he bent over a clear pool for a drink and saw his own face. From that moment he was trapped, staring longingly at his reflection and burning with love. He, too, pined away.

When death eventually took Narcissus, Echo was helpless to reach out to him until he breathed his last. As he said his final "Farewell, farewell" to his own image, she repeated those same words.

Much has been written about narcissism, and perhaps it is appropriate that discussions of the myth have focused almost exclusively on the character who has come to represent pathological self-centeredness. People who consider themselves superior to others are labeled "narcissistic," and there is a certain percentage of narcissistic individuals who harbor such overblown self-images. In my experience, however, this is not the case for the majority.

It is far more useful to view narcissism as a *disorder of bonding*. Narcissists have considerable difficulty forming strong human connections *except when they see aspects of their own personality mirrored in others*. Bonding with independent, autonomous individuals is virtually impossible for them. The right "chemistry" exists only with those who have the same basic values, feelings, needs, attitudes, fashion sense, taste, whatever. And the more they have in common, the tighter the bond can be.

While this may appear to support the theory that all narcissists judge themselves to be superior, many, in fact, suffer from *low* self-esteem. They seek relief by finding people in whom they can see themselves.

In the myth, it was Echo who most affected Narcissus. When other maidens expressed their love for him, he remained unmoved. But when Echo showed how like him she was — her words were his words exactly — he was clearly touched. He responded with one of humankind's deepest emotions: disgust. Nothing disgusts us more than those parts of ourselves we have rejected! He claimed that he would rather die than give her power over him, something she had never asked for. It was the closest he had come to forming a relationship, and the only reason it happened was because Echo mirrored him so perfectly.

Our standard nomenclature for psychological disorders recognizes narcissism as a condition that can cripple an individual's emotional life. It makes sense to take Echo's dilemma equally seriously. If there are people in the world who are limited to bonding with others like themselves, it stands to reason that there are also people ready and willing to serve as mirrors for them. We in the CD field know them as co-dependents.

Freud recognized this complementary role to narcissism when he wrote that "...one person's narcissism has a great attraction for those others who have renounced part of their own narcissism and are seeking after object-love."[1] Echo sought to win Narcissus' affections by giving him back his own words with enough of a twist to suit her purpose. She engaged in a double manipulation — of Narcissus, and of herself. Lost in the process was any sense of what *she* really wanted to say, and she was left with a profound sense of powerlessness. Yet, paradoxically, she had more power over Narcissus than the other, more independent maidens. *Power through sacrifice of self lies at the core of co-dependence.* But the ultimate price is revealed in Echo's fate. At the end, all that was left was her voice, and not even that was under her control.

---

[1]Sigmund Freud, "On Narcissism: An Introduction (1914)," in *General Psychological Theory* (New York: Collier Books, 1963), p. 70.

PART ONE

DEFINING CO-DEPENDENCE

Since one of the major roadblocks to understanding, diagnosing, and treating co-dependence has been the lack of a generally accepted definition of it, I propose the following:

Co-dependence is a recognizable pattern of personality traits, predictably found within most members of chemically dependent families, which are capable of creating sufficient dysfunction to warrant the diagnosis of Mixed Personality Disorder as outlined in DSM III.

Before we go on to list the characteristic traits of co-dependence, we must first surmount two obstacles which have contributed to the confusion now surrounding the term. The first has to do with the different *levels of meaning* with which co-dependence has been associated; the second, with the *competing theoretical frameworks* from which existing definitions have stemmed.

Levels of Meaning

Is co-dependence a didactic tool, a psychological concept, or a disease entity? It has been used on each of these three levels, and we must differentiate among them before formulating any diagnostic criteria.

Co-Dependence as a Didactic Tool

In dealing directly with family members of chemical dependents, co-dependence is used as an important didactic tool. The word itself legitimizes many of the feelings family members have and gives them permission to begin focusing on their own dysfunctional behaviors.

Co-dependence implies that family members have their own "something" to recover from. Its value in direct client education is sufficient reason for mental health professionals to take co-dependence seriously.

Many definitions for co-dependence have developed precisely because of their empirical value in dealing with clients in denial. In reality, such definitions rarely go beyond metaphoric descriptions designed for maximum emotional impact. For example, Charles Alexander characterizes co-dependence as being like a lifeguard on a crowded beach, knowing you can't swim, and hesitating to tell anyone for fear of starting a panic.[1] When confronted with such a description, many co-dependent clients are amazed to discover that anyone else might have an idea of their internal sense of dilemma and desperation.

It is likely that co-dependence will long be a valuable therapeutic tool, especially in the CD field.

Co-Dependence as a Psychological Concept

Psychological concepts such as defense mechanisms, the ego, homeostasis, and enmeshment are useful abstractions. They enable therapists and clinical theoreticians to organize the raw data of human behavior into coherent frameworks, enhance communication about psychological phenomena, and suggest potentially valuable research and treatment approaches.

Whether or not co-dependence is eventually found to be a specific personality disorder, it will likely remain an important concept precisely because it serves these same purposes for CD professionals. In this it is closely related to Melanie Klein's theory of "projective identification" (*see pages 103-104*). Viewed in this light, co-dependence becomes a highly sophisticated psychological concept deserving of further consideration.

Co-Dependence as a Disease Entity

For the purposes of clinical assessment of individual clients, co-dependence can best be seen as a disease entity. CD therapists speak of family members as being affected by co-dependence, or as being actively co-dependent. Such assessments imply that a consistent pattern of traits and behaviors is recognizable across individuals, and that these traits and behaviors can create significant dysfunction. In other words, co-dependence is used to describe a "disease entity," just as phobia, narcissistic personality disorder, and Post-Traumatic Stress Disorder (PTSD) are diagnostic entities.

To date, no criteria have been agreed upon for assessing whether a client is co-dependent. Without such criteria, no standards exist for assessing the presence and depth of pathology, for developing appropriate treatment plans, or for evaluating the effectiveness of therapy. Treatment team members are hindered in their efforts to communicate clearly and understandably about specific clients, and comparison studies of co-dependence are not possible. Unless we can begin gathering reliable and valid research data, co-dependence will remain confined to clinical impression and anecdote.

If co-dependence is truly a disease, then the development of diagnostic criteria will set the stage for sufficient research to document and describe it with scientific clarity, and to conduct treatment outcome studies.

⊏⊐ Competing Theoretical Frameworks ⊏⊐

While discussions of co-dependence have been hampered by its use on at least three levels of discourse, remaining clear about whether we are discussing a didactic tool, a psychological concept, or a disease is only part of the battle. Even within a discussion restricted to one or the other of these, additional problems are caused by the existence of competing theoretical frameworks. This is the second obstacle we must surmount on our way to clarity.

While the origins of the term "co-dependence" are obscure, it is likely that it evolved from "co-alcoholic" when alcoholism and other drug dependencies began being lumped together under the generic "chemical dependence." In any event, the more generic term became common parlance in the CD field fairly quickly. Before long, lots of people were speaking of co-dependence as a disease, but everyone had his or her own definition of it. While these definitions appear to point to the same entity, they do not add up to form a clear picture.

A brief review of some of these definitions reveals that they stem from competing theoretical frameworks, and some intermix frameworks freely.

- *Family systems* approaches, including those advocated by the Johnson Institute and others, attempt to unearth and catalogue the unspoken rules that govern chemically dependent families. For example, Claudia Black's three rules, "Don't talk. Don't trust. Don't feel," codify the tacit prohibitions against speaking honestly about the problem and/or one's feelings. Those who want to be accepted into the family must obey these rules or they are treated as deviants, even though their "deviant" behavior might be healthier than the family norm.[2]

- Outlining the implicit rules governing a family's interactions is one possible systems approach. Another is to identify roles which the family system allows. Earnie Larsen has described six such roles: Caretaker, People-Pleaser, Workaholic, Martyr, Perfectionist, and Tap Dancer. These roles are seen as "self-defeating *behaviors*, greatly exaggerated and complicated by a pathological relationship to a chemically dependent person...that diminish our capacity to initiate or participate in loving relationships."[3]

- Robin Norwood begins with an interpersonal framework when she defines a co-alcoholic as "someone who has developed an unhealthy pattern of relating to others as a result of having been closely involved with someone with the disease of alcoholism." She then combines this definition with primarily intrapsychic symptoms, such as low self-esteem, a need to be needed, a strong urge to change and control others, and a willingness to suffer.[4]

- John Friel, Robert Subby, and Linda Friel venture into *ego psychology*. They contend that adherence to the dysfunctional rules of chemically dependent families eventually leads to identity disturbances within family members. Once a family member has begun investing more psychological energy in his or her false self than true self, co-dependence has taken on a life of its own and no longer needs to be in the presence of a dysfunctional family system to be active.[5]

- Charles Whitfield, whose training is in internal medicine, takes a *behavioral* tack. He describes co-dependence as a primary illness with a recognizable, diagnosable, and treatable range of symptoms and a chronic and progressive prognosis — just like chemical dependence. In the medical tradition, the first concern is in reliably describing the symptoms and course

of the illness, with etiology and treatment coming afterward.[6]
- Perhaps the most global definition of co-dependence has been put forward by Anne Wilson Schaef. She describes co-dependence as a "disease that has many forms and expressions and that grows out of a disease process that is inherent in the system in which we live." She calls this underlying disease process the "addictive process," defining addiction broadly as "any substance or process we feel we have to lie about." The addictive process is tantamount to Freud's death instinct, for Schaef sees it as "progressively death-oriented." Manifestations of the addictive process include chemical dependence, eating disorders, co-dependence, character disorders, and sexism. Clearly, her approach has expanded into social commentary and uses addiction as a sociological metaphor.[7]
- Sharon Wegscheider-Cruse has provided perhaps the most operational definition of co-dependence to date. She combines *behavioral and intrapsychic* elements into a definition which also resembles prevailing definitions of chemical dependence. She describes it as "a specific condition that is characterized by preoccupation and extreme dependence (emotionally, socially, and sometimes physically) on a person or object. Eventually, this dependence on another person becomes a pathological condition that affects the co-dependent in all other relationships." The condition of co-dependence, she maintains, is characterized by delusions/denial, compulsions, frozen feelings, low self-esteem, and stress-related medical complications.[8]

What is common to most of these definitions is the assumption that co-dependence exists independently within members of chemically dependent families, and that many of its manifestations become more overt in the context of a committed relationship — especially with another co-dependent or chemical dependent. These are important insights.

There is something else these definitions have in common: Professionals outside the chemical dependence field have tended to ignore them. To date, they have not been woven into an integrated conceptual framework, nor have they been empirically tested.

One widely accepted framework we do have at our disposal is that of DSM-III. While DSM-III does not provide a general theory of psychology, it does serve three useful purposes: it gives therapists a way to communicate, it provides diagnostic criteria for research, and it affords a means for individual clients to interface with health resource providers. Since all three purposes are of importance to mental health workers, it makes sense to use this framework as a starting-point in our search for diagnostic criteria for co-dependence.

---

[1] Charles Alexander, "The Definition of Co-Dependence," panel at the San Francisco Conference on Children of Alcoholics, The National Association for Children of Alcoholics, July 11, 1985.

[2] Claudia Black, Ph.D., *It Will Never Happen to Me* (Denver: M.A.C Printing and Publications Division, 1981).

[3] Earnie Larsen, *Stage II Recovery: Life Beyond Addiction* (Minneapolis: Winston Press, 1985).

[4] Robin Norwood, *Women Who Love Too Much* (Los Angeles: Jeremy P. Tarcher, Inc., 1985), p. 47.

[5] John Friel, Ph.D., Robert Subby, M.A., and Linda Friel, M.A., *Co-dependence and the Search for Identity* (Pompano Beach, Florida: Health Communications, Inc., 1984).

[6] Charles Whitfield, M.D., "Co-Alcoholism: Recognizing a Treatable Disease," *Family and Community Health* 7 (Summer 1984), pp. 16-25.

[7] Anne Wilson Schaef, *Co-Dependence: Misunderstood — Mistreated* (Minneapolis: Winston Press, 1986).

[8] Sharon Wegscheider-Cruse, *Choicemaking* (Pompano Beach, Florida: Health Communications Inc., 1985).

PART TWO

DIAGNOSING CO-DEPENDENCE

A major roadblock to including co-dependence in any diagnostic nomenclature has been its apparent ubiquity. Described by some as "a condition of the 20th Century," co-dependence is often dismissed as social commentary. If nearly everyone appears to be co-dependent, the argument goes, then how can it be considered a disease?

The answer lies in DSM-III's distinction between personality *traits* and personality *disorders*, a distinction which is directly applicable to co-dependence.

According to DSM-III, personality traits are "enduring patterns of perceiving, relating to, and thinking about the environment and oneself...exhibited in a wide range of important social and personal contexts."[1] Personality traits only become disorders when they are "inflexible and maladaptive and cause either significant impairment in social or occupational functioning or significant subjective distress."[2]

Personality disorders are "generally recognizable by the time of adolescence or earlier and continue throughout most of adult life." Although there is less certainty in diagnosing Personality Disorder in children or adolescents, in some instances maladaptive personality traits may be of sufficient duration (at least one year) to warrant a diagnosis.

The critical point for our purposes is that while co-dependent traits may be widespread, *the diagnosis of Co-Dependent Personality Disorder can only be made in the face of identifiable dysfunction resulting from excessive rigidity or intensity associated with these traits.* Similarly, narcissism is a nearly universal human trait, but Narcissistic Personality Disorder only exists in the face of objective dysfunction. There seems to be no reason why the same line of reasoning cannot be applied to co-dependence.

What remains to be proved through clinical research is whether family members of chemical dependents do in fact develop a recognizable and diagnosable pattern of personality characteristics, and whether these characteristics can become sufficiently "inflexible and maladaptive" as to produce objective dysfunction or significant subjective distress. Here again, such research cannot be conducted until diagnostic criteria for co-dependence have been articulated.

Thus I propose the following such criteria in the style of DSM-III. They place co-dependence within the framework of Mixed Personality Disorder, a condition that exists when an individual does not qualify for a single Personality Disorder diagnosis but has marked traits of several of the Personality Disorders. Since most members of chemically dependent families exhibit a recognizable and predictable pattern of traits, and since this fits our definition of co-dependence, we can begin using these criteria to diagnose the presence of Co-Dependent Personality Disorder.

Let's start by simply listing the criteria. We will then go on to explore and illustrate each.

Diagnostic Criteria for Co-Dependent Personality Disorder

A. Continued investment of self-esteem in the ability to control both oneself and others in the face of serious adverse consequences.
B. Assumption of responsibility for meeting others' needs to the exclusion of acknowledging one's own.
C. Anxiety and boundary distortions around intimacy and separation.
D. Enmeshment in relationships with personality disordered, chemically dependent, other co-dependent, and/or impulse disordered individuals.
E. Three or more of the following:
    1. Excessive reliance on denial
    2. Constriction of emotions (with or without dramatic outbursts)
    3. Depression
    4. Hypervigilance
    5. Compulsions
    6. Anxiety
    7. Substance abuse
    8. Has been (or is) the victim of recurrent physical or sexual abuse
    9. Stress-related medical illnesses
    10. Has remained in a primary relationship with an active substance abuser for at least two years without seeking outside help.

Criterion A:
Continued investment of self-esteem in the ability to control oneself and others in the face of serious adverse consequences.

This criterion is actually an umbrella for a complex set of behaviors and viewpoints which combines many of the characteristics found in Alcohol Dependence (303.9x) and Dependent Personality Disorder (301.60). It encompasses four distinct elements: a *distorted relationship to willpower*, a *confusion of identities*, *denial*, and *low self-esteem*.

Distorted relationship to willpower.

Like chemical dependents, co-dependents believe that it is possible to control their lives by sheer force of will. Chemical dependents show this by repeated efforts to control their drinking or drug use ("I *know* I can stop after one drink." Or, "I swear, I'll never take another drink again"). Co-dependents show it by repeated efforts to control the feelings and behavior of the chemical dependent, as well as their own feelings and behavior ("If only we all try hard enough and pull *together*, we can get your father to stop drinking").

In both cases, the end result is isolation — from others, from their own authentic selves, and from their spiritual and unconscious resources. It becomes an either/or situation: *either* they continue to rely totally on willpower, *or* they succumb to utter hopelessness. There is nothing in between.

It is important to understand the distinction between will*ful*ness and will*ing*ness. The willful person believes that all manner of things can be controlled if one's willpower is strong enough and focused enough. Failure (even failure to control events beyond anyone's ability to control) leads to a sense of inadequacy. The willing person, on the other hand, recognizes the value of determination in those areas where it is possible to exercise influence or control while accepting the fact that there are some things he or she simply can't do anything about. The willing person knows that there are situations beyond any mortal's control, and that everyone has limitations.

Confusion of identities.
Of all the standard Personality Disorder diagnoses, co-dependence comes closest to Dependent Personality. But there are important differences between co-dependence and excessive dependence. One difference lies in the distorted relationship to willpower found at the core of co-dependence and outlined above. Another lies in the confusion of identities which invariably exists in active co-dependents. The co-dependent has crossed a line that other dependent types have not crossed.

When one person becomes dependent upon another, he or she gives that person power over one or more aspects of his or her life. What usually results is a sort of *inter-dependence*. The two strike implied "bargains": "I'll take care of the kids, and you'll put food on the table and pay the rent." If either partner fails to uphold his or her end of a bargain, the other person suffers. But his or her sense of self remains relatively unaffected.

When the line is crossed into co-dependence, that sense of self is compromised and even lost. A *confusion of identities* occurs. The co-dependent's self-worth rises or falls with his or her partner's success or failure. It is as if the partner has become a "barometer" signaling how the co-dependent should feel and behave. (If the co-dependent is not in a relationship, he or she feels an internal void; half of nothing is nothing.)

Now picture what happens when this confusion of identities is combined with the belief that one can control almost anything with willpower. In order for the co-dependent to feel good, his or her partner must be happy and behave in appropriate ways. If the partner is not happy, the co-dependent feels responsible for *making* him or her happy. If the partner is drinking or using drugs (in other words, behaving inappropriately), the co-dependent feels responsible for *making* him or her stop. All of this becomes a matter of intense personal importance. And all of it is perceived as achievable, if only one puts enough effort into it.

Denial.

To continue using alcohol and/or drugs in the face of obviously negative physical, social, and emotional consequences, the chemical dependent must construct a pervasive system of denial. So, too, must the co-dependent. And both go about it in the same way: by suppression, repression, rationalization, and projection.

Uncomfortable facts and feelings ("This marriage is not working," "Her drinking is clearly not normal") are resisted. They are consciously pushed out of one's awareness (suppression). Or they are filtered out of awareness before they even have a chance to rise into the light of consciousness (repression). Or reasonable causes for their existence are substituted for actual causes (rationalization — for example, believing that one got drunk because of being tired, rather than because of how much one drank). Or the cause of one's problems can be seen as lying outside oneself, rather than in one's own behavior (projection).

At the core of the chemical dependent's world is the prideful insistence that he or she can use and keep using without incurring lasting harm. As long as this belief remains unchallenged (in fact, it is unchallengeable — even sacrosanct), then every misfortune and discomfort must be assigned the next most logical explanation. The mutual consistencies among these explanations become part of the fabric of denial, an opaque curtain that conceals reality.

The co-dependent also maintains an unchallenged (and unchallengeable) core belief: that he or she ought to be able to change his or her partner's behavior. When the partner behaves appropriately, this is seen as proof of success. When the partner behaves inappropriately, this is seen as proof of failure due to inadequacy. In either case, the co-dependent perceives himself or herself as playing a central role, and one that has the potential to be quite powerful.

The perception of the self in this role, like the perception of the self as being able to use drugs or alcohol with impunity, requires a fabric of denial. The co-dependent either chooses not to see the chemical dependent's inappropriate behavior or rationalizes his or her own failure to keep the person from using. In the latter case, the failure is attributed to not having tried long enough or hard enough, or to having tried the wrong way. Personalizing the failure offers hope that increasing one's efforts can keep things from getting further out of control.

Thus the denial of the chemical dependent and the denial of the co-dependent are the same. Both work to preserve the status quo, since denial is inconsistent with recovery. And each legitimizes and reinforces the other. Until the pain of continued denial outweighs anxieties about recovery (if it ever does), the chemical dependent will continue to use and the co-dependent will continue to feel responsible.

Low self-esteem.

Most healthy people avoid entering into a relationship with an active co-dependent. As a result, co-dependents are often left with some very poor choices as far as partners are concerned.

If one is going to tie one's self-worth to another person's behavior, it would be best to find a high-functioning, successful partner. But high-functioning, successful people are not likely to want to carry the burden a co-dependent expects them to carry. This burden may be disguised as sincere caring, loyalty, or martyrdom, but the healthy person will not be fooled for long. What the co-dependent is really saying is, "Tell me how to feel and act. When you're sad, I'll be sad. When you're happy, I'll be happy. My self-esteem is in your hands." What healthy person would accept such power?

With their options severely limited, co-dependents usually end up with people with strong narcissistic needs to feel special — such as active chemical dependents. Unfortunately, chemical dependents are bad bets when it comes to taking care of someone else's self-esteem. There is no one more apt to disappoint the co-dependent than the unrecovering chemical dependent. As the disease progresses, the co-dependent's self-esteem is virtually guaranteed to end up as a bust.

We can see how the four elements of Criterion A interlock and strengthen one another. The distorted relationship to willpower leads the co-dependent to try to keep his or her partner happy and sober. The confusion of identities makes doing so imperative. Denial conceals the futility of such a strategy and prevents the co-dependent from seeing the negative consequences of persisting in it. Self-esteem plummets, the sense of inadequacy skyrockets, and the exercise of still more willpower seems like the only recourse.

Unfortunately, as co-dependents urge themselves to try even harder, their efforts to control the situation are often supported by neighbors, relatives, doctors, spiritual advisors, therapists, and society at large. Intervention in the denial system of co-dependents is the exception rather than the rule.

Criterion B:
Assumption of responsibility for meeting others' needs to the exclusion of acknowledging one's own.

Partner: "What would you like to do tonight?"
Co-dependent: "I don't know. What would *you* like to do?"
Partner: "How about a movie?"
Co-dependent: "That sounds nice."
Partner: "Do you have any preference?"
Co-dependent: "Whatever you choose is fine with me."

This conversation appears benign, but the subjective realities for the co-dependent are deeply self-destructive. *Everyone has preferences, however subtle, about nearly everything.* Professing not to care when one is asked to state a preference is fundamentally dishonest. It is not being "flexible," it is not being "polite," it is not the simple act of generosity it might seem on the surface. If the co-dependent were going to a movie alone, there would be little hesitation about making a choice.

But making a choice within the context of a relationship means taking a concrete stand, and that implies risk. To the co-dependent, it is preferable to attend a movie one has no interest in than to risk having one's partner not enjoy himself or herself.

Assuming responsibility for meeting others' needs to the exclusion of acknowledging one's own is a classic symptom of Dependent Personality Disorder. At its root is the fear of being alone or abandoned, which is so great that violence against one's own needs is tolerated. Gradually the co-dependent loses the ability to distinguish his or her needs from those of the other person. He or she takes on the wants and desires of the other in a series of desperate compromises, and the denial system becomes more opaque. Denial of the self for the sake of feeling connected to others is a hallmark of co-dependence. It creates a profound void within the self.

Counterphobic behavior is the other side of the coin. (To understand counterphobic behavior, think of a baseball game. It doesn't matter whether one is at bat or out in the field; the same set of rules still applies.) The co-dependent who *avoids* relationships with others is suffering essentially the same disorder as the co-dependent who ignores his or her needs in favor of a partner's. Rather than take the chance of being abandoned, he or she goes one step further and refuses to get involved at all. In a similar vein, there are teetotalers who remain as tightly focused on alcohol as active alcoholics.

The rules of co-dependence seem to dictate that relating to another person is incompatible with relating to one's own needs and feelings. As a result, co-dependents tend to choose one extreme or another: denial of themselves to keep someone else happy, or compulsive avoidance of others to keep themselves safe.

Criterion C: Anxiety and boundary distortions around intimacy and separation.

The co-dependent equates closeness with compliance and intimacy with fusion. As he or she becomes more involved with another person, the tendency is to take on many of that person's values, wishes, dreams, and characteristics, and eventually much of his or her denial system. The co-dependent becomes a mirror.

Picking up on others' feelings is rationalized as being "sensitive." The co-dependent involved with a chemical dependent actually feels that person's pain, rather than feeling empathy for the pain. This helps to fill the void which results from not honoring one's own needs and feelings.

Anxiety and boundary distortions are experienced most

intensely in the absence of an external structure that defines interpersonal relationships. (An example of such a structure is the work environment, in which relationships and roles are clearly defined.) Without this structure the members of any relationship must continually participate in a mutual negotiation of the interpersonal distance between themselves. When the interpersonal distance decreases, the co-dependent's grasp on his or her true self becomes even more tenuous. When it increases, the co-dependent fears total abandonment, and consequently the loss of the false self he or she has created for the relationship. *Any shift in the status quo will be seen as a threat to the co-dependent's identity.*

When the interpersonal distance between the co-dependent and others changes, the co-dependent may exhibit intense Borderline Personality Disorder characteristics. There may be rapid swings between seeing one's partner as all good or all bad as the co-dependent lurches back and forth between feeling totally inadequate and feeling in control of matters. As black-and-white thinking increases, the world is split into friends and enemies. Friends are often those who support the co-dependent's denial and commiserate with their pain; such friends often are idealized. Enemies are often those who insist on speaking the truth, and they may become the target of intense rage. Impulsive and desperate efforts to regain control of one's world frequently occur. The co-dependent further neglects his or her own needs and can become overtly self-destructive. The anxiety created by changing interpersonal distance can spiral into fear of abandonment or of being overwhelmed by intimacy. All of these factors contribute to relationships being particularly problematic for co-dependents.

The clinical distinction between overt Borderline Personality Disorder and active co-dependence is often hazy and may take more than one interview to evaluate. Over time, the borderline will be seen to lack the ego strength to maintain stable boundaries without the support of external structure. In contrast, the co-dependent does possess the necessary ego strength but voluntarily *dismantles* his or her ego boundaries in an effort to strengthen connections with others. ("If you want to be close, tell me what I should be feeling.") Of course, dual diagnosis can also exist — the same individual can exhibit both Borderline and Co-Dependent Personality Disorders — which further complicates matters. Clarifying the dynamics underlying a particular client's boundary distortions often requires a thorough diagnostic evaluation spanning several sessions.

Criterion D:
Enmeshment in relationships with personality disordered, chemically dependent, other co-dependent, and/or impulse disordered individuals.

According to George Vaillant, writing in *Adaptation to Life*, the defense mechanisms we all use to lessen the distress felt in relationships are constantly maturing.[3] Those of childhood (e.g., magical thinking) gradually give way to those more appropriate to the teen years (e.g., projection, rationalization, and denial) and ultimately ripen into their mature forms (e.g., altruism and sublimation). The failure of these defense mechanisms to develop beyond the adolescent stage is frequently seen in chemical dependents and persons with character or impulse disorders.

Vaillant maintains that it is an almost universal human characteristic to overpersonalize the behavior of someone with the immature defenses of projection, rationalization, and denial. That helps explain the hurt and anger most people feel when trying to relate to the chemical dependent or sociopath. Maintaining direct human contact with such a person eventually becomes intolerable — unless one is co-dependent, in which case one accepts the projections, contributes to the rationalizations, and supports the denial. In other words, when the co-dependent is confronted with immature defenses in others, he or she responds by mirroring them.

There are other reasons for this mutual attraction. Criterion A notes the tendency of the co-dependent to give others power over his or her self-esteem. But not everyone wants that sort of power over another person, and those who do usually possess a narcissistic need to be considered special. Chemical dependents in the active phase of their disease, and persons with personality or impulse disorders, have this need. Thus a complementary situation exists, one in which the co-dependent and the chemically dependent, personality disordered, or impulse disordered person can find mutual gratification without ever having to express their needs overtly. They call it "chemistry." They fall in love!

Unfortunately, the chemically dependent, personality disordered, or impulse disordered person is not the ideal caretaker for one's self-esteem. When the inevitable happens and the co-dependent's self-esteem is dashed, the co-dependent responds with a pledge to redouble his or her willpower and make it work next time.

Criterion E:
Three or more of the following:

Co-dependence is similar to chemical dependence in a number of ways. Both are diseases of denial, and both exhibit a wide range of symptoms.

Any chemical dependent can point to certain symptoms of that disease which he or she does not display; the unrecovering chemical dependent may then use such "evidence" to shore up his or her faulty denial system. Co-dependents can display a wide enough range of symptoms that no single individual could have them all; some of the symptoms even seem contradictory. In addition, co-dependents who are still in denial frequently ignore symptoms which are obviously present while focusing on those symptoms they do not display. Such "negative" evidence is cited as proof that they are not co-dependent. To the CD professional, this whole process is seen as further evidence of denial, which is a prime symptom of active co-dependence.

1. Excessive reliance on denial.

The denial of co-dependence and the denial of chemical dependence are virtually indistinguishable. Each represents a selective inattention to internal and external realities.

Denial lies largely *outside* the direct control of a person's conscious awareness. It results from a deep unwillingness to experience feelings that would ensue if those forbidden realities were acknowledged — an unwillingness so deep that the mind blocks any awareness that would lead to these dangerous emotions. It is a very active, if unconscious, process, requiring the constant input of psychic energy to scan the environment so "blinders" can quickly be activated.

Denial may be seen as an impaired strategy for achieving security. In the face of a threat, narrowing one's awareness can create the appearance of safety. A *global* constriction of awareness would be *psychotic* denial; the denial of co-dependence and chemical dependence is more selective, excluding awareness of threatening realities while admitting others.

If a threat can be ignored, then one doesn't have to take any action to ameliorate or avoid it. But one must be constantly vigilant. As a result, the need to deny compounds over time and may eventually reach a point where the psyche can't maintain.

Co-dependents frequently see the breakdown of their denial system as a sign of their own personal inadequacy, much as chemical dependents view their growing lack of control over their using as a sign of personal weakness. Each typically attempts to regain control through renewed applications of willpower.

Paradoxically, the recovering person reacts to a threat in quite the opposite way — by *expanding* his or her awareness. This allows him or her to more accurately assess the level of danger and, if possible, take effective action.

For active chemical and co-dependents, however, denial continues to give the false impression of security. It is rarely acknowledged and relinquished until the pain and emptiness of their ever narrower and more isolated life becomes too much to bear.

2. *Constriction of emotions (with or without dramatic outbursts).*

Co-dependents frequently view emotions as enemies (or as weapons). Many families in the early stages of treatment mistakenly believe that they must curb their emotions and not allow them to affect their behavior or relationships. This becomes a test of willpower, a way to prove that they are able to maintain at least a semblance of control over their lives.

Typically, the emotions they work hardest to restrict are those normally considered to be immature, dangerous, uncomfortable, or just plain bad: anger, fear, sadness, rage, embarrassment, bitterness, loneliness, etc. Unfortunately, it is impossible to put a lid on such "negative" feelings without also impeding the expression of more positive ones, such as happiness. Co-dependents tend to use perhaps 30 percent of their emotional energy to cage another 30 percent they have deemed undesirable. That leaves only 40 percent of their emotional energy free and available to them — not much with which to enjoy a full, rich, and gratifying life. Peggy Lee put it best in her musical lament, "Is That All There Is?"

This effort to control one's feelings is precisely the behavior targeted by the second half of A.A.'s First Step: "We admitted... that our lives had become unmanageable." Co-dependents are deeply dedicated to "managing" their lives — a dedication which stems from the same *hubris* which leads humans to feel that they can improve on nature by exterminating dangerous beasts or by throwing poison on fields to eliminate "bad" insects. Sooner or later the entire ecosystem reacts to such uses of brute force, and the consequences can come from unexpected directions. By killing the beetles on our crops, we poison the birds that eat the beetles and also keep the mouse population in check. Suddenly the mice are free to devour the crops. The lesson to be learned here (and we're not learning it very quickly) is that complex systems like the ecosystem cannot be "managed" to suit our goals without becoming less healthy.

The meadows of our emotional landscape are equally complex. When one part attempts to "manage" the whole, our general emotional makeup suffers. We cannot improve our lives by stifling undesirable emotions, any more than we can improve ecosystems by eradicating or exterminating selected elements.

A typical phenomenon in co-dependence is the tendency to resort to the more extreme mechanisms of dissociation or depersonalization. In a desperate attempt to survive (in other words, not to feel), they will "close down," "shut down," "phase out," or go into a spontaneous trance. This results in a quality of being more present in body than in mind. Clients in therapy can actually be seen to separate themselves from the intensity of the moment. Their facial expressions become fixed, they seem to gaze off into the distance, their breathing grows shallow. These are signs that they have clicked into their "survival mode" and are allowing the world to wash past them. Numbness gives the illusion of safety and control.

Co-dependents may also exhibit symptoms which appear to directly contradict the constriction of feelings: the dramatic outburst, and the compulsive exposure of feelings.

When unexperienced feelings have built up over time, the most minor incident can trigger an explosion. An unpleasant feeling will resonate with a backlog of similar feelings, and the effect will be inappropriately intense. For example, a co-dependent who is reluctant to express his or her feelings about a spouse's drinking might blow up at a friend who forgets to send a birthday card. Or a torrent of rage might follow a relatively insignificant act of thoughtlessness on the part of the spouse. In any event, the co-dependent is left feeling "crazy" and "bad."

Note that the outburst is directed at a "safe" — or at least safer — target. It's not the forgetful friend who is the *real* problem, it's the spouse's drinking. Ironically, the very intensity of the outburst will be used as an excuse for discounting it.

The compulsive exposure of feelings is an effective disguise for constricted feelings. Some co-dependents go to great lengths to verbalize *every* feeling as soon as it enters their awareness. They also pressure those around them to continuously expose *their* feelings. While such behavior might appear to be the opposite of the emotional "constipation" so often seen, its purpose is essentially the same: to avoid having to deal with feelings or experience them any longer than necessary.

The essence of co-dependence is to minimize the anxiety and ambiguity of allowing feelings to run their natural course, whether by damming them up or by expelling them as quickly as possible.

3. *Depression.*

Anger turned inward, unresolved grief, the chronic restraint of feelings, being identified more with one's false self than one's true self — co-dependents have plenty of reasons to be depressed. Typically, however, they view their depression as evidence of inadequacy and the failure to stay in control, and for this reason they usually deny its presence. To acknowledge depression is to acknowledge loss, which challenges the family's shared denial and focuses attention on one's own feelings.

Co-dependents often cite the pressures of children, work, and home life as justification for not indulging in their personal feelings. ("Too many people depend on me to be there for them.") Admitting that one is depressed means admitting that one has needs, and co-dependents, by definition, always place the needs of others above their own in importance. For therapists to work effectively with co-dependents, they must be able to recognize the presence of depression despite the clients' inability to confirm that observation.

For children who spend their developmental years in chemically or co-dependent families, depression stems from actual *deprivation* rather than loss; a bond which never existed cannot be loosened. Children naturally protect themselves from unstable bonds, and in those who develop co-dependent traits while their personalities are still forming, depression may become characterologic and normalized. Acknowledging their depression requires that they develop new levels of trust in others — a difficult task at best, since their early experience has taught them that their trust will not be reciprocated or respected.

4. *Hypervigilance.*

The co-dependent's environment is unpredictable, basically incomprehensible, and highly stressful. Active chemical dependents bring chaos into the very fabric of their personalities and family interactions, and those around them can never predict what they will do next. Decisions that are 95 percent made can be randomly reversed or ignored. The only way for the co-dependent to survive is by being ultra-sensitive to subtle shifts in the chemical dependent's behavior and mood.

Such hypervigilance is a recognized symptom of Post Traumatic Stress Disorder (PTSD), which is most typically seen in combat veterans. By putting his vigilance on automatic pilot, a soldier is always prepared to react. Unfortunately, there is seldom an "off" switch. Once a co-dependent starts scanning the environment for signs of impending disaster, a state of free-floating anxiety can be established.

Hypervigilance is also a natural byproduct of investing one's self-esteem in another person's behavior. To feel good about himself or herself, the co-dependent must first attend to everyone else's happiness. The merest hint of dissatisfaction in another signals that one's own behavior needs to be modified. In order to control how others feel and behave — the co-dependent's goal in life — it is essential to stay on one's toes and catch inappropriate behavior in its earliest stages.

Of course, hypervigilance requires great expenditures of energy. When the strain becomes too much to bear, the co-dependent may suddenly feel overwhelmed and demoralized. Episodes of apathy can alternate with frenetic efforts to monitor everything and maintain control.

5. Compulsions.

Compulsivity is a primary defense process. The object of a compulsion is of secondary importance and often changes over time. A recovering chemical dependent may pass through periods of compulsive eating, compulsive spending, compulsive working, and compulsive relationships after achieving abstinence. The internal dynamic is always the same: a struggle between two poles, one "inside" and one "outside." The person's identity is connected to resisting the impulse, while the impulse itself is experienced as an alien force. The resulting high drama distracts the person from unwanted feelings, which usually have little or nothing to do with whatever compulsion is currently occupying center stage.

Like chemical dependents, co-dependents can only remain active in their disease by disregarding the pain that it brings.

Unlike chemical dependents, however, co-dependents have no biochemical "booster" for their denial system. For them, compulsions serve the same purpose, whether the compulsion is to eat, to work, to rescue others, to watch television, to read, to seek sex, to gamble, to be religious, whatever. Many co-dependents can describe in detail the subjective experience of sliding gradually into the whirlpool of their compulsivity. There is a surge of adrenaline. An intense buildup of emotions specific to the compulsion occurs ("I've *got* to stop eating"), while more threatening emotions are eclipsed ("I feel empty in this marriage"). A feeling of inevitability takes over. Eventually they stop resisting the compulsion, and this is followed by a temporary sense of relief.

In most cases, the emotions that are being avoided are unavailable for the duration of the compulsion. In order for the emotions to surface, be identified, and be experienced, one must abstain from the compulsion. This is another way in which the co-dependent and the chemical dependent are similar: to recover, both must choose abstinence.

6. *Anxiety.*

The anxiety of co-dependence can take a variety of forms, from free-floating, chronic anxiety to panic attacks, phobias, and existential dread. Some of this anxiety is in response to the random chaos inherent in living with an active chemical dependent. It becomes free-floating because of the generally high level of denial the co-dependent must maintain. In some cases, that denial blocks the co-dependent from acknowledging that the chemical dependence even exists; in other cases, it protects the co-dependent from having to face up to the level of stress he or she is living under. When one is able to remain unaware of that level of stress and its source, the anxiety appears "sourceless" and free-floating and is perceived as still another sign of personal inadequacy.

While the deep existential dread that co-dependents experience often goes unrecognized, therapists can use it as an avenue for making an important empathic connection. Co-dependent anxiety reaches this stage for two reasons. First, when one's self-worth must continually be validated by someone else, there is an ever-present risk that one's identity will be thrown into limbo should the relationship come to an end. (As one depressed widow said, "I used to be half of something wonderful. Now I'm half of nothing, and half of nothing *is* nothing.") Second, co-dependents are by nature chameleons. They become whatever their partners want and need them to be. But mirroring the actions and emotions of others means abandoning one's true self in favor of a facade — a false self. And even this false self must shift and change according to others' needs.

Gradually the true self becomes less and less substantial, until the anxiety the co-dependent is feeling becomes *anxiety about his or her very existence*. When one devotes more emotional energy to one's false self than one's true self, there is a genuine risk of emotional death. This is what the co-dependent senses, even if he or she can't articulate it.

7. Substance abuse.

Co-dependence is a setup for the development of chemical dependence. When one habitually responds to threats by denying that they exist (in other words, by narrowing one's awareness), the use of mood-altering chemicals is a logical next step. Denial is necessary to avoid being overwhelmed by feelings, and substance abuse serves as a biochemical "booster" for one's crumbling denial. In short, *substance abuse is consistent with the personality structure of the co-dependent.*

As noted earlier, co-dependents exhibit a wide range of compulsions, and the use of alcohol or drugs falls into this category. Traditionally, however, the co-dependent who compulsively uses chemicals in the service of denial is diagnosed as being *chemically dependent*. This is as it should be; when chemical dependence is present, it must always be treated as the primary issue. *But it cannot be seen as the only issue.* Once the chemical dependence has been broken, the co-dependence remains; left untreated, it acts as a barrier to long-term sobriety.

In *I'll Quit Tomorrow*, Vernon Johnson described the "ism" of alcoholism as being the same illness as co-dependence when he wrote, "The only difference between the alcoholic and the spouse, in instances where the latter does not drink, is that one is physically affected by alcohol; otherwise both have all the symptoms."[4] If this "ism" goes untreated in a chemical dependent who stops using alcohol or drugs, he or she is considered to be "dry." Being dry is a setup for relapse. Similarly, an overwhelmed denial system is a setup for turning to substance abuse. It is not at all unusual for a co-dependent to become harmfully involved with alcohol or drugs following a divorce, or the death or recovery of the chemical dependent.

Helping professionals tend to view chemical dependence and co-dependence as two distinct problems and apply different labels to their symptoms. The denial of the chemical dependent is termed "alcoholic thinking," "drug mentality," or "stinking thinking," while the denial of the co-dependent is called "co-dependent thinking" or "co-ing." In fact, these divisions are largely artificial. The denial of the chemical dependent and the denial of the co-dependent are cut from the same cloth. The disease of chemical dependence and the disease of co-dependence largely overlap. And often the person who has one will have the other as well. While it is probably rash to say that *all* chemical dependents are also co-dependent, we can safely assume that active co-dependence is at least as common among chemical dependents as it is among their family members. (This may be true in part because fully *half* of all chemical dependents have at least one chemically dependent parent they have had to relate to.)

When a co-dependent is also chemically dependent, the latter must be treated first. But the underlying co-dependence must not be ignored.

8. Has been (or is) the victim of recurrent physical or sexual abuse.

In many chemically dependent families, the threat of physical and/or sexual abuse is always present. Whether it stems from abusive incidents or merely from feeling like a hostage to the angry rantings or depressed ruminations of an out-of-control spouse or parent, it lodges in the heart like a thorn.

All too often these incidents, rantings, or ruminations occur during a blackout. When the next morning comes, the chemical dependent has no memory of them and, accordingly, feels no guilt. Meanwhile the rest of the family stays caught up in the fear from the night before. They hide their emotions, but for the rest of the day — and often for weeks and months to come — they work anxiously to keep the threat from coming true.

Co-dependents tend to minimize both the amount of violence in their relationships and the level of stress they live under. They do not see themselves as victims of physical or sexual abuse except in the most extreme cases, and even then they frequently take the blame: either they "caused" the abuse, or they "deserve" to be treated abusively. Especially if few or no overtly abusive acts have occurred, the co-dependent's denial system prevents him or her from viewing the situation realistically. As one co-dependent said (in all earnestness), "My husband is good to me. Whenever he hits me, he only uses his hand. He never uses a board or anything that could do any real damage."

In extreme cases, co-dependents remain in relationships in which they are chronically abused. While it may be difficult to understand how anyone could live this way for any amount of time, it is important to realize that co-dependents perceive their experience from a distorted — and self-reinforcing — point of view. When others are unhappy, they see it as a result of their own inadequacy, and being abused further lowers their self-esteem. As often happens in hostage situations, they begin to identify with their aggressors and empathize with their aggressors' frustrations and disappointments. Their own needs take second place or are not considered at all. In the end, they stop believing that they should be treated with respect. They simply can't conceive of living any differently than they are.

The victims of physical and sexual abuse are usually too embarrassed to speak freely about it. In such cases the therapist must become a gentle but persistent advocate for the client — a delicate balancing act requiring considerable skill and sensitivity. For co-dependents to speak honestly about being abused, they must develop a level of trust in the therapeutic alliance which exceeds what they think they are capable of. Telling the truth requires them to "betray" their family, and the resulting sense of guilt may activate the tendency to minimize what they have just said. Or it may release a flood of dammed-up feelings. For a time, they may be overwhelmed by grief and rage — feelings which must be fully experienced for the co-dependent to have any chance of seeing how and why the abusive relationship has developed, and how it can be changed.

Physical and sexual abuse take on more ominous dimensions when they are perpetrated upon children, who are frequently unaware that what is happening to them is wrong and *not their fault*. These buried feelings and ancient betrayals accompany them into adulthood. We now know that abuse is cyclical, and that many of its victims grow up to become abusive themselves. But even those who do not are still damaged. Many co-dependents who become the victims of recurrent abuse are caught up in a forgotten pattern which was established long ago. They never verbalized their feelings then and are reluctant (or unable) to do so as adults, which is why the therapist's role is potentially so important. By taking seriously the client's buried feelings, the CD professional can create the first safe environment the client has ever known in which to explore and deal with them.

Chemical dependence is such a common contributor to physical and sexual abuse that its presence should always be considered. One of the most reliable symptoms of co-dependence is the inability to leave a chronically abusive relationship behind, whether that relationship is ongoing or past.

9. Stress-related medical illnesses.

Family members of chemical dependents require greater than average amounts of medical care — not for the somatic equivalents of emotional distress, but for what are generally considered to be stress-related medical illnesses.[5]

A co-dependent's home life is highly stressful. Compounding this constant exposure to stress is the co-dependent's way of dealing with it: by denying that it exists, and/or by denying that one is affected by it. In the short run, this strategy seems to work. The co-dependent is capable of getting through times that might slow down or stop people with less determination or willpower. This in itself becomes a source of pride, which serves to offset the co-dependent's chronically low self-esteem.

Unfortunately, the body is not so easily fooled. Although the co-dependent may remain unaware of the toll that the stress is taking on him or her, this does not change the fact that the body is under attack. After a decade (or two, or three), parts start breaking down in ways that can no longer be denied. Conditions that are either created or exacerbated by stress include headaches (tension and migraine), asthma, hypertension, stroke, gastritis, peptic ulcer, spastic colon, rheumatoid arthritis, and sexual dysfunction. The role of stress in a host of other physical conditions is a subject of legitimate debate. While the jury is still out on these, it is a fact that stress-related illnesses *do* exist and are found more frequently in people with dysfunctional reactions to stress, such as co-dependents.

In treating stress-related illnesses, it is common medical practice to prescribe increasingly more powerful medications, or to add tranquilizers. But in many cases co-dependent patients do not respond. In such cases, the most powerful prescription might be a direct referral to Al-Anon. Joining Al-Anon can be the first step toward learning how to respond differently to the stress one is experiencing. By modifying their awareness of when stress is or is not present, co-dependents can often begin responding to treatments which work for other medical patients.

Although co-dependence is not as dramatically or directly life-threatening as chemical dependence, it is potentially just as fatal. The progression into chemical dependence, suicide, violent or accidental death, and death due to untreated stress-related illnesses can all be tied to co-dependence. Since the minimization of one's co-dependence (or the minimization of *oneself*) is a symptom of the disease, it is difficult to get the co-dependent to look honestly at his or her situation. One way to break through this denial is to confront co-dependents with the life-threatening medical consequences of living with stress.

10. Has remained in a primary relationship with an active substance abuser for at least two years without seeking outside help.

Co-dependents come up with endless reasons for not seeking outside support, and many sound more than reasonable. No one likes to admit that their family is incapable of solving its own problems. No one wants to expose their family to the scrutiny of others.

But there is a point at which these reasons become excuses, and the desire to stand on one's own two feet becomes martyrdom. When one refuses to seek outside support to avoid having one's denial system confronted, silence has become self-serving. When one is motivated by fear of the chemical dependent, the situation is no longer healthy. When one is blocked by pride, passivity has become dangerously self-destructive.

How can we tell when this point has been reached? How can we be sure that failure to seek help is a manifestation of active co-dependence, and not simply a normal urge to handle one's problems in one's own way? When should we stop giving co-dependents the benefit of the doubt? I propose an arbitrary time period of two years, after which the co-dependent's motives automatically become suspect. Whether this is an appropriate length of time is open to debate. But there *must* come a day when the burden is placed on the co-dependent to prove that his or her actions are not contributing significantly to the problems he or she is trying to hide.

In other words, if a co-dependent has lived for two years with an active chemical dependent without initiating his or her own recovery program or doing an intervention, the presumption of active co-dependence should be made.

Two years seems long enough for family members to acknowledge the presence of chemical dependence, if they are at all open to facing the truth. It is also long enough to realize the impossibility of trying to live a normal life in the abnormal environment of a chemically dependent family.

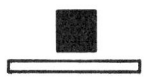

In the end, whether co-dependence is seen as a disease or not depends to a considerable degree on how one defines a disease. Nonpsychotic Psychological Disorders are generally *patterns of maladaptive behavior which lie outside an individual's conscious ability to control* (e.g., phobias, depression, personality disorders). In this broad sense, co-dependence can be seen as a true disease, as outlined by the criteria described above.

Co-Dependent Variants

As noted previously, the signs and symptoms of co-dependence are so comprehensive and diverse that no individual will display every one. Co-dependents who are still in denial will often point to aspects of the disease which do not "fit" them, using such negative evidence to "prove" that they are not co-dependent or to minimize the extent of their co-dependence.

There are, however, constellations of certain behaviors that are often seen in co-dependents. Co-dependents can often identify with a specific variant more than with the more general diagnosis of co-dependence. To the professional's eye, all these variants are seen as being different expressions of the same underlying issues.

The Martyr

This may be the most common manifestation of co-dependence. It is probably safe to say that all co-dependents have something of the martyr in them.

Martyrs operate primarily on false pride. They take great pleasure from their capacity to put up with inconvenience, disappointment, even pain. They derive their self-worth from being able to fight the battle as much as from winning or losing. Martyrs deem it more important to be "right" than to be effective.

Many chemical dependents exhibit the equivalent of co-dependent martyrdom: they, too, are committed to solving their problems on their own. Both bear their burdens with a stiff upper lip. In return, they feel that their noble behavior is deserving of others' respect — and, in fact, their family members and friends do tend to perceive them as tolerant, long-suffering, and generous (sometimes to a fault).

But behind this impressive front lie some unwelcome truths. Martyrs feel that they live as they do because *they have no choice.* The alternatives are too frightening to consider: leaving and being on their own, or confronting the situation and being left and on their own. They keep sacrificing themselves in the hope that their investment will eventually pay off, but even this is something of which they cannot be sure.

Martyrs feel empty inside, but they are usually so busy being martyrs that they have little or no time to experience that emptiness and what it means.

The Persecutor

The opposite of the martyr is the persecutor. Persecutors harbor much of the rage and bitterness which martyrs cannot allow themselves to feel. Although their own behavior often seems out of control, they focus on what everyone else is doing wrong. Rather than dealing with their unhappiness, they externalize it and blame it on the actions of others.

While martyrs take full responsibility for feeling miserable, persecutors take *no* responsibility for theirs. While martyrs push themselves to work harder to feel better, persecutors push *others* to provide them with security and peace of mind.

Both overestimate the impact they have on those around them. Neither knows the difference between what they can and cannot control. The martyr keeps trying to manipulate others by being good; the persecutor keeps trying to manipulate others with anger and guilt.

The Co-Conspirator

Some co-dependents continually undermine chemical dependents' efforts to attain sobriety. Although this seems counterproductive from the outside, it can make sense from within the co-dependent's world.

Co-dependents become attached to the identities they develop within the actively chemically dependent family system. The thought of having to develop a new identity — a requirement for functioning within a recovering family — causes considerable anxiety. Rather than change, they become co-conspirators, or *enablers.*

Enabling behaviors are those which support chemical dependents' efforts to deny or conceal their illness. The underlying motives do not matter; it is the end result that counts. The most profound enabling occurs when the co-conspirator continues to deny that the chemical dependence even exists. This denial can be so severe that it goes on long after the chemical dependent has entered treatment.

Most co-conspirators are offended by the mere suggestion that a family member might have a problem. It is a painful irony that many co-conspirators become professionals in the CD field out of concern for the harm that drugs and alcohol are doing to this country and to family life in general. The words "in general" are key to understanding this phenomenon. Co-conspirators know that chemical dependence is a "bad thing"; they simply aren't willing to recognize its presence close to home.

Some co-conspirators are capable of acknowledging that a family member is chemically dependent, and even of expressing concern about that person. But then they turn around and offer him or her a drink, or volunteer to stop at the store to buy more alcohol! When confronted with the inconsistency of their behavior, they deny that it is contributing to the problem or claim that they can't act any differently. ("What choice do I have? He's going to drink anyway, whether I buy it or he does.")

The Drinking (or Drugging) Partner

As noted earlier, co-dependents are at risk for becoming chemically dependent. Their lifestyle and belief system are already so close to those of chemical dependence that it is easy to slip into addiction. Many co-dependents believe that the best way to "connect" with a chemically dependent family member is by joining in. Eventually they become chemically dependent as well.

Sometimes the co-dependent's eyes are opened when he or she simply can't keep up with the chemical dependent's consumption of alcohol or drugs. This is the point at which a healthy person would start confronting the chemical dependent with this knowledge. For active co-dependents, however, this is too risky. Instead, they back off on their own using and bury their heads in the sand, hoping that the chemical dependent will someday do the same.

The Apathetic Co-dependent

Some co-dependents simply stop caring. They become so thoroughly demoralized that they sink into an emotional stupor, like concentration camp inmates resigned to their fate. Apathy may bring a certain peace or calm, but it is devoid of any sense of hope or meaning in life.

This is especially distressing when there are children in the home. When Dad or Mom gives up, there is no one left to model healthy responses to the chaos and insanity of living with chemical dependence.

For the therapist, this situation is especially challenging. When the co-dependent becomes apathetic, one of the major avenues to building a therapeutic alliance is effectively blocked. The therapist cannot suggest that dealing with the problem will bring an end to pain because the co-dependent no longer feels much pain. Furthermore, he or she never wants to again. Thus every effort to rekindle hope within the co-dependent is ignored or resented, because allowing oneself to hope not only feels foolish but also leaves one open to pain.

For severely apathetic co-dependents, suicide becomes a realistic and acceptable option. They may take their own lives actively and directly, or passively and indirectly — by doing nothing to avoid an accident, for example, or by refusing to see a doctor at the onset of disease.

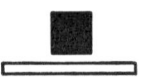

What is important to realize is that co-dependence wears many faces. Doubtless there are other variants than those described above. And there are no "rules" determining which ones co-dependents may manifest and when: the martyr may become the persecutor, the co-conspirator may become apathetic, and so on.

Oversimplification of the concept is an ever-present danger, and describing "typical" behaviors or roles is a sure way of falling into that trap. I have presented the most common variants solely as illustrations. The absence of any (or all) of these recognizable variants should not be taken as evidence that co-dependence does not exist.

Clinical Examples and Transgenerational Diagrams

Let's put some clinical meat on the theoretical bones outlined above. The following examples are designed to suggest the variety of clinical situations when the diagnosis of co-dependence might be appropriate. Example I illustrates individual therapy; example II, family therapy; and example III, a medical practice. Example IV shows two different transgenerational diagrams and demonstrates the usefulness of this history-taking tool, which is often employed during treatment center intake.

I. The Unrecovering Family Member in Individual Therapy

Mildred, a 52-year-old woman, sought therapy because she feared that her alcoholic husband, Jack, was about to relapse after 12 years of continuous sobriety. Although the initial focus was on family therapy, it soon became apparent that Jack was present only out of concern for Mildred's symptoms of chronic depression and anxiety, panic attacks, and near-phobic avoidance of social situations. Jack's sobriety seemed secure, but Mildred kept insisting that he was on a dry drunk. The marriage was strained predominantly because Mildred's own life was out of control.

Mildred was terrified that Jack would abandon her again by resuming his drinking. Her depression was a sort of anticipatory grieving process. Avoiding social situations was one way to minimize the likelihood that Jack would be exposed to alcohol and tempted to use it. As it turned out, alcohol was more of a concern for Mildred than for Jack.

Once Mildred was able to focus on her own fears and poor self-image, she agreed to enter group therapy before pursuing couples work any further. Eventually the therapy revealed memories of her paternal grandfather, who had moved into her parents' home after being widowed when Mildred was three years old. For the next ten years, her grandfather went on drinking binges, and finally died of cirrhosis of the liver at age 58. Her father was so ashamed of her grandfather that he became a rigid, and often vocal, abstainer.

In time, Mildred was able to articulate how she had felt as she watched her grandfather slip away. At that point she began to let go of her current fears that Jack was bound to drink again.

Comments: This case illustrates the effect of unrecovering co-dependence on a couple where the chemically dependent partner has successfully entered recovery. Because Mildred stayed focused on alcohol even after Jack stopped drinking, she was unable to find an inner sense of freedom once Jack's sobriety was established. Her symptoms prevented the growth of intimacy with her husband (Criterion C), and she continued to sacrifice much of her life (Criterion B) to what she perceived as Jack's ongoing need to be protected from alcohol (Criterion A).

Mildred exhibited denial, constriction of emotions, depression, compulsions, and anxiety — all of which fall under our Criterion E. Her exposure during childhood to the loss of a parental figure to the disease of alcoholism meant that her co-dependence was probably deeply ingrained.

II. Family Therapy in Early Recovery

Most family therapists in the CD field will recognize the following scene:

A couple and their child sit in silence as you enter the room. None makes eye contact with you, although one (or all) might be trying almost desperately. The man has his arms crossed over his chest, is red in the face, and seems ready to bite anything that moves. The woman looks woebegone, with her head hanging and a tear poised to fall from the corner of her eye. The child's feet are flailing about under the chair; if the chair were pulled out from under him, the child would probably hit the floor running.

As painful, as extreme, as poignant as this picture may be, it is reminiscent of many chemically dependent families you have seen before. Your task, should you choose to accept it, is to interact with the family, help each person clarify his or her own motivation (or lack of it) for being a member of that family, and maximize the chances that a functional family system will emerge if they choose to stay together.

You turn to the man. The veins in his neck are prominent and seem to pulse even harder whenever he holds his breath or speaks. You thank him for coming. He stares at you. You ask how he is feeling and he booms, "Fine...I'm feeling fine since the drinking stopped." You ask how it feels to be at a family therapy session, and he scowls and replies, "I don't see why it's necessary to talk about our private lives in public. We're doing okay, and this can only stir up trouble." (Or you may hear any one of several versions of the same thing. Some people will intellectualize; some will be charming; others will glower and glare. Underneath all of these behaviors will be fear and anger.)

You comment to the man that he appears to be irritated. He barks back, "I'm fine." It is clear that you are not being invited to pursue that line of conversation any further.

You turn to the woman. She seems to shrink slightly under your gaze, but mostly she looks sad — terribly sad. As empathically as possible, you ask how she is feeling. She sighs before saying, slowly and painfully, "I guess...I've been feeling... really good, now that the drinking has stopped." You remark that she looks very sad. She glances at her husband, who quickly averts his eyes — a simple transaction loaded with meaning and perfected over years of practice. Before you can comment on it, she goes on to say, "No, really...I'm doing a lot better." She, too, has chosen to remain closed to you.

You turn to the child, who fidgets more than ever. When you say that it is nice to meet him, he lets loose with a torrent of words: "Things have been fine since the drinking stopped/Last weekend we all went out for a family picnic/Everyone drank Pepsi/It was really fun...." When you start to suggest that the child might be a bit nervous, he denies it before you finish your sentence. The mother reaches for the child's hand, but it is immediately withdrawn and held behind the chair.

Comments: Everyone is "fine" — except that everyone isn't. All three family members are exhibiting the same behaviors. All are either unaware of their feelings, incapable of labeling them (denial and constriction of feelings), or unwilling to speak honestly about them (Criterion A). All are choosing to remain hidden. No one is making personal contact — with you, or with anyone else in the room (Criterion C).

Co-dependence is active in all three, including whichever one also happens to be chemically dependent. The whole family is invested in denying their feelings, in feeling responsible for how the others are feeling (Criterion B), and in attaching their self-worth to the facade that everything is "fine." The party line becomes each individual's official feelings (Criterion D).

This vignette illustrates how a dry chemical dependent and an unrecovering co-dependent can be indistinguishable.

III. Failure to Respond to Appropriate Therapy for Stress-Related Illness

Martin, a 45-year-old-man, has been treated over a span of three years for mild hypertension (an average blood pressure of 142/94). At his physician's urging he lost 10 pounds, but he is still about 20 pounds overweight. He has begun exercising but rarely works out more than once a week. He has complied with his doctor's recommendations in all other ways — eating a low-salt, low-fat diet, and taking antihypertensive medications.

Because Martin's blood pressure has been remarkably resistant to treatment, his physician has escalated from diuretics to beta-adrenergic blocking agents, and to alpha-methyldopa and hydralazine (for trial periods). A full medical evaluation has not yielded any new information or insights. Over the three years in question, Martin has also suffered from intermittent gastritis, for which antacids have proved only marginally helpful.

Martin's physician has gathered sufficient psychosocial data to learn that his patient drinks very little alcohol and uses no other psychoactive drugs. Martin is principal of a large high school, which is a source both of constant stress and of deep satisfaction. He denies having any family problems.

One day Martin comes in for a routine checkup and is seen by the physician's partner, a recovering alcoholic. He immediately notices several things about Martin that his regular physician had not been aware of. Martin is unwilling to "take the doctor's valuable time" to talk about himself (Criterion B). He seems unwilling to discuss his emotional life, especially when asked about being depressed. He acknowledges some compulsivity in his eating and especially in his work habits (Criterion E). Although he admits that he is frequently anxious about his work (he is concerned with pleasing parents and meeting his superintendent's expectations), he quickly downplays the amount of stress he is under (Criterion A). He tends to confuse personal and professional elements in his relationships with the teachers under his supervision, especially those who are most manipulative (Criteria C and D).

The physician goes on to take an expanded family history, with a focus on drug dependence. Martin reluctantly identifies his father, his paternal grandfather, and several aunts and uncles on both sides of his family as alcoholics. He denies that this history has had any affect on him and resists exploring it any further, but briefly becomes teary-eyed and allows a moment of more personal contact with the physician.

The doctor senses that Martin has more that he needs to say but cannot be pushed at the moment. He prescribes attendance at an Al-Anon meeting emphasizing adult children of alcoholics, as well as a general Al-Anon Family Meeting, and gives Martin a list of possibilities.

Within six months Martin's regular physician is able to reduce the dosage of antihypertensive medications. As a result of regular attendance at Al-Anon meetings, Martin has become able to speak openly for the first time about his fears that his wife may be alcoholic. As his recovery progresses he becomes more sensitive to the stresses of his job and better able to manage his stress level. He eventually asks his physician's partner for a referral to someone in the local community who can assist him in intervening on his wife's secret but self-destructive drinking and tranquilizer abuse.

Comments: Once a person learns to recognize the signs and symptoms of co-dependence, it becomes remarkably easy to see them in others. The criteria highlight clinical data which must be considered meaningful until proven otherwise.

On the other hand, *unwillingness* to pay attention and respond to evidence of co-dependence may be a sign of active co-dependence on the part of the observer. The observer may be assumed to be participating in the same denial as the co-dependent.

IV. Transgenerational Diagrams

William is an alcoholic. In taking a history of alcoholism in William's family, the following diagram was developed:

DIAGNOSING CO-DEPENDENCE

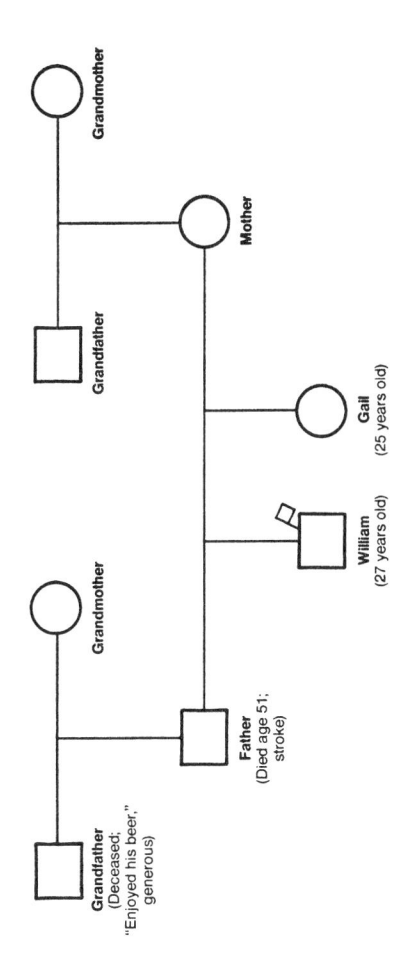

Grandmother

Grandfather

Mother

Grandmother

Grandfather
(Deceased;
"Enjoyed his beer,"
generous)

Father
(Died age 51;
stroke)

William
(27 years old)

Gail
(25 years old)

At first glance, the alcoholism seems to exist as an isolated event. For example, William describes his late paternal grandfather as "a man who enjoyed his beer," but this is quickly followed by stories about how generous and much loved he was.

An entirely different picture emerges if the diagram is fleshed out to include all chemical dependence, co-dependence, compulsive behaviors, and stress-related medical problems within the family, and if we assume that all chemical dependents are also co-dependent. William's family tree now looks like this:

DIAGNOSING CO-DEPENDENCE

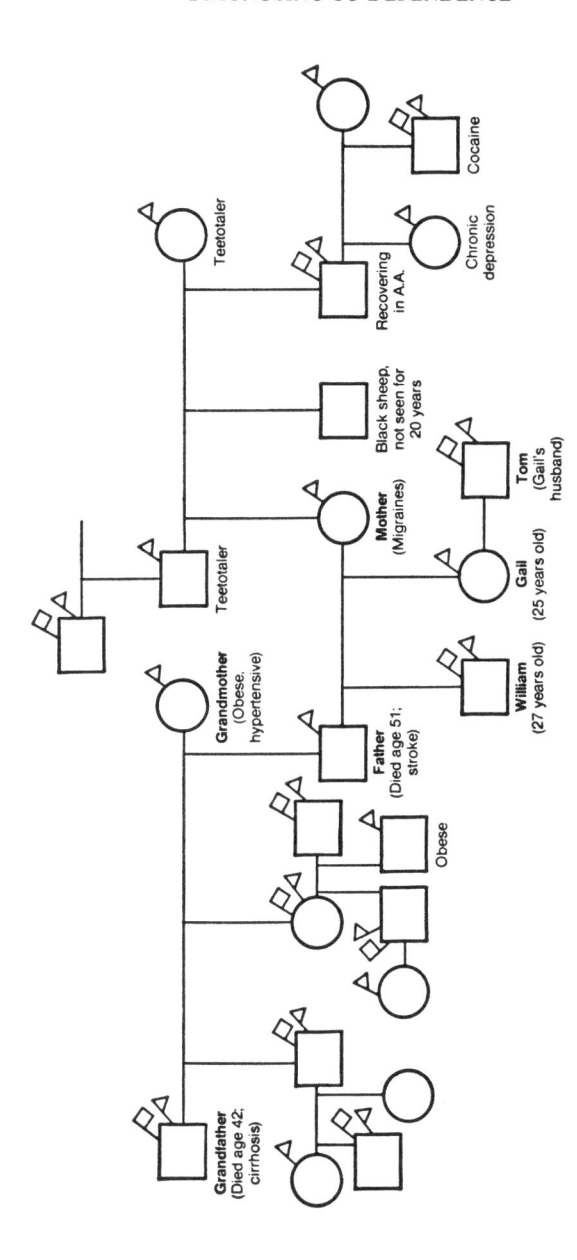

Square flags represent chemical dependence; triangular flags represent co-dependence. (These symbols follow a convention first used by Sharon Wegscheider-Cruse in her work at the Johnson Institute.)

Comments: Even a cursory glance now reveals that this family has been deeply affected by the disease of chemical dependence for generations. Few members have escaped completely, and new recruits (spouses, children, etc.) are always coming in.

Transgenerational diagrams demonstrate graphically how chemical dependence can disrupt whole families, and how co-dependence can be transmitted to offspring. Co-dependence is both a disease in and of itself, and one of the vectors for transmitting chemical dependence. William's chemical dependence no longer is an isolated event, and his co-dependence has not skipped any generations.

"Co-ing" vs. Helping

The diagnostic criteria outlined above are useful for evaluating whether an individual's overall pattern of behavior indicates the presence of co-dependent personality disorder. But what about *specific* behaviors or actions? Clinicians are often faced with the problem of having to determine whether a given behavior is a manifestation of co-dependence or an expression of normal concern. This puzzle can only be resolved by establishing a framework for distinguishing "co-ing" from helping.

This does not necessarily simplify things, however. First, the same behavior can be an example of *either* co-ing or helping, which means that it is not enough to look at behavior alone. We must also consider the context from which it has sprung — the *motivation* behind the behavior. Second, even co-dependents are capable of helping, and it is not true that anything they do must be co-ing by definition. People are extraordinarily complex. Co-dependents are capable of being helpful, and certainly therapists and other helping professionals are capable of co-ing.

Diagnostic criteria for co-dependence can help in determining whether a particular act leans more toward co-ing or helping. I condense the criteria into three axes and apply each axis to the act. Depending on where the act falls along these axes, we can be fairly certain whether it represents co-ing or helping behavior. Of course, in the real world, most actions will be a mixture of both. The axes suggested below help determine whether one or the other is predominant.

Axis A: Relationship to Willpower

To what degree is an individual acting in order to gain a sense of pride in what he or she is capable of making happen? To what degree is he or she involved in trying to control the world beyond realistic limits? When it seems likely that an individual is gaining self-esteem by forcing solutions by dint of willpower, he or she is probably co-ing rather than helping. When an action is overly willful, it is usually co-ing.

For example, an individual might plan a surprise birthday party for his or her spouse. When the motivation is primarily the pleasure of orchestrating the event, seeing it come together, and enjoying the spouse's reaction, the action may be considered to be helpful. But when the motivation is the desire to control how the spouse celebrates his or her birthday (by not serving any alcohol, by inviting only non-drinking friends, and so on), then the action is more likely co-ing.

Axis B: Relationship to Personal Needs

To what degree has an individual acted to meet someone else's needs rather than his or her own? Or, if the individual has acted in line with his or her own needs, how much guilt is he or she feeling as a result? Many acts of kindness are performed out of a sense of obligation. If this sense of obligation is a cause for resentment, then the actions may be considered co-ing.

For example, a parent might leave work early and skip an important meeting in order to attend a child's Little League game. If the parent secretly resents having missed the meeting, or if he or she is feeling ill and really needs to get home to bed, attending the game is not the generous and loving act it seems. Pretending that it is a simple act and that there will be no repercussions from having ignored one's own needs represents co-ing.

Axis C: Level of Autonomy

What does the act imply about the individual's separateness from — or fusion with — others? Has he or she acted out of choice or the compulsion to earn others' approval? Behaviors that appear utterly selfless can signal trouble. When a person feels bound to be kind in order to keep others happy and avoid the risk of being abandoned, it is likely that he or she is co-ing.

For example, a wife might sacrifice long-held plans to visit her family when her husband is asked to serve as United Way Chairman during the time they originally planned to be away. On the surface this may look like a supportive (and admirable) decision. But is there any real reason for the wife to stay at home? Can't she visit her family on her own? Or does she fear that her husband's drinking will get out of hand if she is not there to control it? The "sacrifice" here was explored in therapy and eventually seen to result from the wife's feeling little autonomy from her husband. It was not the simple act of consideration for him that she portrayed it to be. Relating directly to her family, without the protective presence of her husband, was too anxiety provoking, and this was the real reason for cancelling her plans. "Selfless" decisions can be a sign of mature altruism — or they can indicate co-ing behavior.

We can further condense these axes into three simple words: *pride*, *shame*, and *doubt*. Pride refers to one's willfulness; shame, to feelings about one's own needs; and doubt, to uncertainty about who one is when apart from others.

Co-dependents often vacillate between pride and shame, which is both confusing and frustrating for those around them. Because they care so deeply about how others see them, they place great importance on how they *appear*. They develop a facade to use when dealing with the outside world *and* with those they are most intimate with. Because this facade is pleasing to others, it must be protected and maintained at all costs. Eventually they begin to identify emotionally with the facade. Confusion (their own and others') escalates as the false self "replaces" the true self. The false self continues to be shaped by the needs and wishes of others, while the true self becomes the repository for unwanted and unmet personal needs — and, consequently, a source of shame.

The co-dependent's experience thus becomes one of keeping up a front of always being in control. Underneath, however, his or her life is a shambles.

By recognizing that specific behaviors may be either helpful or co-ing, based on the underlying motivations, we remove ourselves from the temptation to apply a cookbook approach to evaluating clients. By applying the axes of pride, shame and doubt, we are exploring the personal *meaning* of any action. This is similar to how a good therapist, in taking a chemical dependence history, focuses not only on the *amount* of drinking and drug use but also inquires into the meaning (i.e., the role it is playing in the individual's emotional life).

Special Concerns with Children and Adult Children of Alcoholics

One view of co-dependence holds that adults are capable of falling into greater and greater dysfunction as a result of being in close relationship to an active alcohol or drug abuser. This view implies that a state of relative health existed before the co-dependence became established. But this is not always the case, particularly for children who grow up around co-dependent and chemically dependent adults. When these are the models a child has, co-dependence can be built right into the fabric of his or her character.

There are substantial risks involved in being raised in a chemically dependent family. Children from such families are over-represented in almost every "casualty" category. The list is impressive: fetal alcohol syndrome, alcohol- and drug-related birth defects, hyperactivity, stuttering, eating disorders, contact with the foster care system, child physical and sexual abuse, school phobias, school dropouts, runaways, contact with the juvenile justice system, teenage pregnancy and prostitution, and early drug and alcohol abuse, to name a few.

However, as Margaret Cork showed in *The Forgotten Children*,[6] not all the damage is so obvious. Much, in fact, is hidden, carried around in youngsters who *appear* normal and have been labeled "invulnerable" when, in fact, their self-esteem and ability to trust others has been seriously affected. This burden can be carried throughout adulthood and is a perfect setup for becoming actively co-dependent or chemically dependent later in life.

It would be nice if growing up in a chemically dependent home somehow immunized children against falling into the same behavior. Unfortunately, people end up doing what they know, and this frequently means traveling the paths that our parents have demonstrated.

Experience with children from chemically dependent homes reveals that many suffer to some degree from symptoms associated with Post-Traumatic Stress Disorder (PTSD) — a disease seen in combat soldiers, most often today in Vietnam veterans. PTSD is not the same as co-dependence, and co-dependence is not the same as PTSD, but the two interact synergistically.

PTSD is believed to occur among people with normal defenses who have been subjected to levels of trauma which clearly lie outside the range of what is considered to be normal human experience (especially if the trauma is chronic, of human origin, and sustained within a closed social system). While it may be a matter for debate whether growing up in a chemically dependent family should be considered "normal human experience," I am personally not willing to accept it as such.

The symptoms of Post-Traumatic Stress Disorder seen in children from chemically dependent homes are described below.

Re-experiencing the Trauma

Once a person has been overwhelmed by traumatic events, he or she is susceptible to the sudden reemergence of the feelings, thoughts, and behaviors that were present during the trauma. This reemergence is most likely to occur when the individual is faced with something which symbolically represents the original trauma — a "trigger." This gives rise to all the survival behaviors that were appropriate at the time — survival behaviors which may well be *in*appropriate at a later date.

For children from chemically dependent families, the trigger can be almost anything: the sound of ice clinking in a glass, an expression of anger or criticism, arguing, the sensation of losing control, etc. The survival behavior they know is active co-dependence: focusing on others' needs to the exclusion of their own, feeling inadequate, exercising ever greater amounts of willpower.

Children from chemically dependent families are often plagued by the sudden reemergence of deeply co-dependent behaviors. This can recur throughout adulthood, even if they reach high levels of maturity and competence in most other areas of their lives.

Psychic Numbing

During moments of extreme stress, combat soldiers are often called upon to act regardless of how they are feeling. Their survival depends upon their ability to suspend feelings in favor of taking steps to ensure their safety. Unfortunately, the resulting "split" between one's self and one's experience does not heal easily. It does not gradually disappear with the passage of time. Until an active process of healing takes place, the individual continues to experience a constriction of feelings, a decreased ability to recognize which feelings are present, and a persistent sense of being cut off from one's surroundings (depersonalization). These add up to a condition known as *psychic numbing*.

The constriction of feelings is a prominent symptom of active co-dependence (Criterion E), and PTSD can increase the severity of whatever co-dependence is present. Anything which symbolizes the out-of-control feelings of growing up in a chemically dependent family will trigger this symptom — because one's parents often broadcast the message that it is not permitted to have feelings. Children from chemically dependent families feel good about being adept at stifling emotions. They learned early that it is useful to have a gulf between oneself and one's emotions.

Hypervigilance

Individuals under the threat of disaster tend to put their vigilance on automatic pilot so they can continually scan the environment for the smallest sign of impending danger. Many Vietnam veterans found, upon returning home, that their automatic pilot did not have an "off" switch. They remained on edge, always expecting the worst, unable to trust or feel safe again.

Even as adults, people from chemically dependent families are unable to feel comfortable unless they are continually monitoring their surroundings. This is superb training for active co-dependence. If an individual is overly reliant on the opinions and feelings of others for his or her own self-esteem, *and* is always watching for the slightest change in their facial expressions or tones of voice, then he or she will be in a constant state of tension. Free-floating anxiety develops. Both hypervigilance and anxiety are associated with co-dependence under Criterion E. Unfortunately for those who grew up in chemically dependent homes, catastrophe really *was* lurking in the wings, and the anticipation of catastrophe is an extremely difficult habit to break.

Survivor Guilt

It is not uncommon for people who survive a traumatic event to feel a sense of guilt. No rational explanation exists for why a piece of shrapnel found one person's chest and spared another. Veterans can carry the burden of survivor guilt for the rest of their days. Whenever they begin to experience the fullness that life has to offer, they immediately feel as if they are betraying those who never had the chance.

Children from chemically dependent families often have great difficulty separating themselves from their parents. It seems somehow wrong to go away and be healthy when those who are left behind are still suffering. It is as if there is an unwritten rule in chemically dependent homes: no one is allowed to become more healthy than the sickest family member.

Individuals from chemically dependent families differ in at least one more respect from adults who have slid into active co-dependence. This has to do with the source of their depression (Criterion E-3).

As Jael Greenleaf points out, depression associated with co-dependence can originate in loss, or in deprivation.[7] To have a relationship with a spouse who later becomes actively chemically dependent is a loss; to be born into a family where one or both parents are already chemically dependent is deprivation. The problem is not that one's trust was broken, but that there was never any reason to start trusting. The problem is not that one sacrificed one's independent identity to stay connected with an addicted parent, but that one never developed an independent identity.

When a child grows up around parents who have no concept of the proper boundaries between individuals, he or she continues to perceive identity as something that is shared. Independence is to be avoided, since it leads to feelings of abandonment and betrayal — burdens too heavy for any child to bear.

At worst, chemically dependent families are breeding grounds for the development of Borderline Personalities. At best, they continue to give rise to succeeding generations of chemical dependents and co-dependents. Not surprisingly, they also give rise to a lot of CD therapists and other helping professionals.

---

[1] American Psychiatric Association, *Diagnostic and Statistical Manual of Mental Disorders*, Third Edition (Washington, D.C.: American Psychological Association, 1980), p. 305.
[2] Ibid.
[3] George E. Vaillant, *Adaptation to Life* (Boston: Little, Brown & Co., 1977).
[4] Vernon E. Johnson, *I'll Quit Tomorrow* (New York: Harper & Row, 1973), p. 30.
[5] J. Lavino, "COAs in the Workplace," presented at the Governor's Conference on Children of Alcoholics, New York, 1982.
[6] R. Margaret Cork, *The Forgotten Children* (Markham, Ontario: Paperjacks, 1969).
[7] Jael Greenleaf, *Co-Alcoholic: Para-Alcoholic* (Los Angeles: The 361 Foundation, 1981).

PART THREE

TREATING CO-DEPENDENCE

Many of the current treatment approaches to co-dependence are somewhat simplistic. This stems largely from a widespread misunderstanding of the nature of the disease. Once we accept that co-dependence exists on a par with other personality disorders — such as borderline, narcissistic, and dependent personalities — it should become clear that it deserves to be treated with the same level of therapeutic sophistication.

In other words, co-dependents need more than four weeks of lectures and discussions to be able to make the required characterological changes. They need in-depth therapy. Historically, treatment for co-dependence has suffered in two distinct ways:

- Therapists trained in traditional mental health approaches have attempted to treat the *symptoms* of co-dependence, diagnosing clients as having anxiety disorders, depression, hysterical personality disorders, or dependent personality disorders, to name a few.

Without the framework of co-dependence to work from, many of the central issues (particularly regarding the misuse of willpower) have not been dealt with. And the results have often been disappointing, similar to treating a chemical dependent's anxiety and depression without dealing directly with his or her chemical abuse.
- Therapists in the CD field have recognized the co-dependence, but are often constrained to approaching it as an adjunct to treating the chemical dependent.

A family education program is valuable, especially one with aftercare designed to help family members connect with a Twelve-Step Program (Al-Anon, Alateen), but it hardly represents the depth of psychodynamic psychotherapy required to treat characterological issues.

Treatment for co-dependence has also been hindered by a failure to distinguish it from family therapy. Although the two are not mutually exclusive, they are distinct. You should *never* assume that the co-dependence of individual family members is being adequately addressed simply because the family is being seen as a whole. Family therapy during early recovery consists primarily of practicing basic family communication and social skills, with the goal of reestablishing appropriate boundaries and increasing the flow of information. These skills are of potential value for any family member who is actively co-dependent, but they hardly constitute intensive therapy for a personality disorder.

General Considerations

There are five important factors to consider before initiating any kind of therapy:
1. whether the client is currently using drugs or alcohol,
2. whether his or her home environment is conducive to recovery,

3. whether the client is suffering from Post-Traumatic Stress Disorder (PTSD),
4. whether individual or group therapy is preferable, and
5. what stage of recovery the client is currently in.

The Current Use of Drugs or Alcohol

If the client presents evidence of chemical dependence, or even of harmful involvement with alcohol or drugs without overt addiction or dependence, the primary thrust of the therapy must focus on this issue. Failure to address chemical abuse (when present) as the primary therapeutic issue incurs an unacceptably high risk of enabling the client's denial system and sending the indirect message that if the other part of his or her life can be straightened out, the abusive use of chemicals will stop.

Attempting to effect significant change in a client who is using chemicals irresponsibly is a Catch-22. For therapy to be successful, the client must be willing to tolerate the increased levels of anxiety that precede significant change. But if the client's characteristic response is to diminish anxiety by increasing his or her consumption of psychoactive chemicals, he or she is engaging in the one behavior which is most likely to defeat therapeutic efforts and protect the status quo. For therapy to have lasting effect, the client must have a drug-free brain.

The Home Environment

If the client's home environment impedes therapy, residential treatment should be strongly considered. Both co-dependents and chemical dependents are especially sensitive to the demands of their surroundings during the early stages of recovery. The concept of detoxification applies not only to the need for chemical dependents to withdraw from the effects of the chemicals they have ingested; it also embraces the need for asylum, for refuge, for protection from the stresses and temptations of an environment which has a stake in the client's *not* recovering.

Under extreme circumstances, it is necessary for co-dependents to separate themselves from their current environment in order to be able to focus enough attention on themselves to get their recovery off the ground. Even under less extreme circumstances, it can still be *useful* for co-dependents to "detox" from the insanity of a chemically dependent family system in order to fully break their denial. Residential treatment for co-dependence is occasionally a necessity, and often an advantage, during the early stages of recovery. There is rarely the need for such treatment to be hospital-based, unless that is the only available option.

The Presence of PTSD

If the client has been sufficiently traumatized by growing up in a chemically dependent home or by being physically abused in a chemically dependent relationship, PTSD may be present. In the face of PTSD, the concept of therapy by catharsis becomes particularly simplistic. Therapists are often tempted to ply their therapeutic "lance" to the boil of submerged emotions. Unfortunately, this only confirms what many PTSD clients fear: that they cannot allow themselves to become aware of their emotions without running the risk of being overwhelmed.

If the client demonstrates full-blown symptoms of PTSD, it is prudent to heed what has been learned in the treatment of Vietnam veterans. Those therapists who work successfully with this population have learned to honor the client's need to keep a lid on his or her feelings. The most effective therapeutic process involves swinging back and forth between uncovering feelings and covering them again, and it is precisely this ability to modulate their feelings that PTSD clients have lost.

Helping them to become comfortable with their feelings again is a lot like teaching teenagers how to drive a car. After showing them how to buckle up, turn on the engine, engage the clutch, put it in gear, and step on the gas, it becomes necessary very quickly to teach them how to use the brakes as well. Without this knowledge, driving a car is a terrifying experience. Successful driving involves the ability to pass back and forth freely between use of the gas pedal and use of the brake pedal.

PTSD clients must feel secure that their ability to close their emotions down will never be taken away from them, but instead will be honored as an important tool for living. The initial goal of therapy here is to help clients move more freely into their feelings with the assurance that they can find distance from them again if they begin to be overwhelmed.

Once children from chemically dependent homes, adult children of alcoholics, and other PTSD clients become confident that you are not going to strip them of their survival mechanisms, they are more likely to allow their feelings to emerge, if only for a moment. And that moment will be a start.

Group Therapy vs. Individual Therapy

Even when both group therapy and individual therapy are available, group is generally the treatment of choice for co-dependents. Because co-dependence tends to be triggered within relationships, group is especially effective at eliciting symptomatic behavior, thus bringing a client's problems into the therapy session. In individual therapy, co-dependents are often capable of honing in on the subtle cues of the therapist and feeding back what they perceive to be "good client" behavior. The multiple relationships within a group cannot be managed as easily, and an environment reminiscent of the family setting develops.

In addition, it is valuable for co-dependents to receive support and validation from peers, not just from the therapist. It becomes a corrective emotional experience for clients to be part of a healthy, recovering "family system," one in which positive feedback is given for breaking denial and speaking the truth about one's feelings and needs.

There are exceptions — clients who are unable to profit from group and are best dealt with individually. For example, some clients are so anxious that they cannot tolerate the pressure of being in the same room with several other people. Other clients end up being disruptive because they are too deeply in denial or are unclear about appropriate boundaries. Still others are so out of touch with their feelings that they cannot even talk about them, much less deal with them. These clients often require the use of experiential techniques (e.g., gestalt and psychodrama) in individual or workshop settings. Finally, clients with dual diagnoses obviously require treatment modalities individually tailored to their specific needs.

The Current Stage of Recovery

The process of recovery can occur spontaneously — in other words, without the help of treatment. Facilitating this process by psychotherapy does not affect the sequence of steps the individual passes through, although it can both speed his or her recovery and extend it more deeply into his or her personality structure.

Professionals hoping to help co-dependents must be familiar with the stages of recovery (outlined in the following section). This is analogous to the need to understand the normal stages of grief if one is going to be of value to a client who seeks therapy following a loss.

Understanding *what* recovery entails is a prerequisite to understanding *how* it occurs and can be augmented by treatment.

Since clients enter therapy during different stages of their recovery, professionals must be able to evaluate their status before they can respond with appropriate therapeutic techniques.

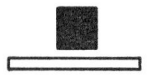

This is a good place to say a few words about referring clients to self-help meetings, such as Al-Anon or Adult Children of Alcoholics groups. *There is really no time in therapy when such referrals are inappropriate.* Meetings provide valuable support and a structured program for advancing one's recovery. In addition, they offer a benefit that even the best therapist cannot: the sense of hope that comes from direct contact with recovering co-dependents.

If clients reject such referrals out of hand, or attend a few meetings and then conclude that "they don't belong there," you should use this information as you would any other type of resistance and thoroughly explore the underlying feelings and reasons. (For chemical dependents and co-dependents alike, there is no better Rorschach than the refusal to attend A.A. or Al-Anon meetings.) The skilled therapist will get most of his or her clients either to attend such meetings or to talk in detail about why they are not attending them.

When you make referrals to meetings based on the Twelve Steps, you should be prepared to conduct the therapy in a manner consistent with them. It is even better if you personalize the program by working its steps on some aspect of your own life — a particular compulsion, perhaps, or detachment from a client toward whom you are overextended.

Given that Twelve Step self-help groups like A.A. and Al-Anon place such strong emphasis on the value of a spiritual life, you should also consider this when designing and conducting therapy. Remain open to hearing about and honoring your clients' spiritual efforts. If only for professional reasons, try coming to terms with your own spiritual impulses, since this will enable you to take a therapeutic stance which is least likely to do violence to those impulses in your clients.

The rediscovery of one's spirituality can lead to the deep characterological change that is essential to recovery from co-dependence. But because my intent is to help professionals to do better *therapy* with co-dependents, I have restricted my comments to the means by which psychotherapy can promote such change with or without the assistance of spiritual efforts on the part of the client. This is not because I believe this approach to be any better or more powerful than the spiritual one; it is simply because I know more about it. I also do not mean to imply .hat the two are inconsistent with each other; indeed, those therapists who take spirituality into account are probably more effective practitioners as a result.

The Stages of Recovery

The recovery from co-dependence and the recovery from chemical dependence are remarkably similar and can be seen to pass through the same four general stages: the *Survival Stage* (Stage I), the *Re-identification Stage* (Stage II), the *Core Issues Stage* (Stage III), and the *Re-integration Stage* (Stage IV).[1] It is not surprising that the two should parallel each other so closely, given (as Vernon Johnson has noted) that the "ism" of alcoholism is shared equally by both the drinking and the nondrinking family members. If the diseases are essentially the same, so, too should be the recovery process.

The Survival Stage (Stage I)

For the chemical dependent, the Survival Stage is marked by blanket denial that an addiction exists. Every effort is made to maintain the illusion that the chemical use is still voluntary. Even abstinence is attempted as proof that one is not addicted.

Denying the existence of addiction requires a lot of fancy mental footwork. All of the negative consequences of drinking or using must be explained away by enormous amounts of rationalization and projection. It is important to acknowledge that the chemical dependent is often more rational than he or she is given credit for being. Many of the rationalizations and projections are actually quite logical, *if one accepts that there is no chemical dependence present* — which the chemical dependent does.

Any attempts to attack this logic are doomed to failure. The only path to recovery lies in confronting the core denial — the belief that one can control behavior and limit one's intake while under the influence of alcohol or drugs. The most effective tool with which to confront this denial is an awareness of the pain that stems from addiction — the pain one feels, and the pain one causes. Helping the chemical dependent to arrive at this awareness is one of the goals of intervention.

It is also important to acknowledge that the chemical dependent's belief that continued use of a chemical is necessary to feel normal is probably not far from the truth. Many chemical dependents experience extreme discomfort during withdrawal. Some have grand mal seizures; others experience high levels of anxiety or profound depression. In the most severe cases, the individual may be convinced that the chemical is necessary for his or her survival, both emotional and physical.

Co-dependents also undergo a Survival Stage characterized by a blanket denial that a problem exists. They deny that chemical dependence is present within their family; they deny that they might be co-dependent; they deny that they feel anything one way or another. They are dedicated to hanging on to their denial and continuing it at any cost. To relinquish it means to jeopardize their identity. They fear this on a primitive, existential level, which explains the ferocity with which co-dependents can fight back when their denial is threatened. The sourceless sense of pain they feel is tolerated as their lot in life.

Like chemical dependents, co-dependents place a premium on maintaining that their behavior is voluntary. While this appears to be in direct contradiction to the compulsivity which runs their lives, it makes sense if it is perceived as a *denial of limitations.* Co-dependents take pride in believing that they can always draw on their willpower to tolerate one more disappointment. This belief creates the illusion that they are in control while everything around them is out of control.

What happens when co-dependents start abstaining from their blanket denial? Although this is not likely to cause the physical symptoms that chemical dependents feel upon withdrawing from alcohol or drugs, it may well exact equally high emotional costs. Valued relationships may be lost, and if one's identity is tied to those relationships the risks involved in recovery are very great indeed.

For both chemical dependents and co-dependents, the initial stages of abstinence would be a lot easier to bear if one could somehow start recovering first! Unfortunately, it doesn't work that way. The only avenue toward recovery requires a leap of faith long before anyone feels ready for it.

The Re-identification Stage (Stage II)

At some point, often born of desperation, the core of the chemical dependent's (or co-dependent's) denial system can be shaken. We know very little about this watershed moment, except that one is more likely to reach it if he or she can somehow become (or be made) aware of the increasing amount of pain in his or her life.

One way this happens is through fortuitous groupings of crises, when many things go wrong (and cause pain) at the same time. Another way it happens is if the person finally "hits bottom" and loses everything (marriage, job, friends, financial position) or tragedy strikes (a car accident, injury to a loved one). Still another is intervention, a process designed to precipitate a crisis at a time when a person still possesses enough physical and emotional resources for recovery to be possible and *before* everything is lost.

Regardless of the means, the result is a crack in the denial system through which the person glimpses his or her true self — a re-identification.

For some individuals, however, the fortuitous grouping of crises never comes. For some, the "bottom" is so far down that it is only reached in death. And for some, the intervention never takes place. The denial system remains intact until the bitter end.

There are two critically important facets to the Re-identification Stage. The first is the *acceptance of a label*; the second is the *acceptance of limitations*.

Accepting a label.

Prior to entering this stage, the chemical dependent is committed to being "normal." Upon re-identification, he or she becomes willing to accept being labeled an alcoholic or a drug addict. These are harsh words, but they are less harsh than the reality with which he or she is faced.

Acknowledging one's chemical dependence yields three positive returns. First, it is a relief to be able to take a more objective view of one's life. Second, a new framework for reinterpreting one's past becomes available. And third, one can actually start looking forward to the future because there is a realistic basis for hope.

Accepting a label isn't easy. Chemical dependents have trouble with this, and so do co-dependents. For the latter, it means forsaking the role of noble martyr or righteous persecutor. It becomes much harder to see oneself as a victim when the label of co-dependent (or adult child of an alcoholic/drug addict) requires that you take responsibility for your own dysfunctional behavior. Like chemical dependents, co-dependents tend to enter re-identification only after being convinced that it is more painful not to. Once they do, however, the rewards are similar. For the first time, the co-dependent can more realistically assess what has happened in the past; for the first time, he or she can anticipate the future with optimism rather than fear. There is a critical willingness to have the future be different.

Accepting one's limitations.
The second important facet of re-identification ties into the second half of the First Step of the Twelve Step Program pioneered by A.A. and Al-Anon: recognizing that one's life has become unmanageable. When one accepts limitations, one can stop attributing this unmanageability to personal inadequacy or insufficient willpower. That, too, is a relief; that, too, absolves one of the past and gives one hope for the future.

Every therapist and CD professional has seen alcoholics or drug addicts whose recovery has never advanced beyond the acceptance of the label. We call this staying "dry." Because they never deal with the "ism" of alcoholism — the way of thinking and feeling that was built around their chemical dependence — they are prime candidates for relapse.

Before they move on to recovery, they must acknowledge the distorted relationship to willpower which has heretofore guided their lives. Only then can they begin investigating the realistic role willpower can play and acknowledging where it can have no effect whatsoever. Like any tool, willpower is useful only for certain things. Trying not to be chemically dependent (or to make someone else happy) by sheer force of will is analogous to trying to pound a nail in with a saw. Saws are just right for some jobs, but they were not built for others — including nail pounding. Similarly, willpower is handy for influencing such things as one's own behavior, but it is totally ineffectual when it comes to influencing another person's emotional world, or one's genetic susceptibility to addiction.

Co-dependents are also capable of accepting the label without going any further — in other words, of staying "dry." As long as they remain in the active phase of their disease, they continue to behave as if all manner of things can be controlled through the exercise of will. When reality proves resistant, they automatically redouble their efforts.

Recovery, in contrast, is heralded by the willingness to explore what is *really* under human control and to accept that much of the universe lies forever outside our ability to influence it by force of will.

Establishing a realistic relationship with willpower is a task that must be undertaken by chemical dependents and co-dependents alike. For this reason, I prefer to view "dry" chemical dependents as those who fail to face their co-dependence issues. This view is consistent with the argument that all family members suffer from the "ism" of alcoholism and avoids creating an arbitrary structural division between chemical dependents and co-dependents.

Traditionally, we have used different words to describe the failure to face these issues. With chemical dependents, we have called it "alcoholic thinking" or "addictive thinking"; with co-dependents, we have called it "co-dependence." By terming it "co-dependence" in all cases, we put all family members in the same boat. This has the beneficial effect of increasing empathy in a situation which needs every scrap of empathy it can get.

The Core Issues Stage (Stage III)

There is usually one critical aspect of a person's life where it becomes clear that any attempt to control what happens is doomed. For the chemical dependent, it is his or her drinking or drug use. For the co-dependent, it is usually his or her efforts to stop the chemical dependent's drinking or drug use.

In either case, recovery begins during the Re-Identification Stage through the process of coming to terms with the limitations of willpower. During the Core Issues Stage, the lessons learned about one's powerlessness are broadened and incorporated into the fabric of one's life, with far-reaching implications.

What we are describing here is the paradox of *winning through losing* — which is just another way of saying that chemical dependents and co-dependents can only move ahead by stepping back. They must abstain from those strategies of willpower which have compounded the problems they were supposed to solve.

The Core Issues Stage is characterized by an increasing willingness to apply this winning-through-losing approach to wider and wider areas of one's life. In particular, recovering persons must eventually face the fact that relationships in general cannot be managed by force of will. Instead, successful relationships require that *each* partner be independent and autonomous.

For co-dependents, this idea goes against the grain. It takes a real leap of faith to stay separate from people with whom you are trying to be intimate!

Carried even further, this "Zen of willpower" also compels the eventual realization that *most* human emotions fall outside the range of one's influence. Not only is it impossible to control other people's emotions; it is downright difficult to control your own. You cannot predict how you will feel about a particular event on a particular day, and neither can you direct yourself to feel a certain way when it happens. The most you can do is to respond honestly to your feelings from one moment to the next, and choose to respond with healthy and appropriate behaviors.

The Core Issues Stage, then, is one of detaching oneself from the struggles of one's life — struggles which exist because of prideful and willful efforts to control those things which are beyond one's power to control.

The Re-integration Stage (Stage IV)

By the time a person passes through the Core Issues Stage and reaches the Re-integration Stage, there is essentially no difference between the recovery process of the chemical dependent and that of the co-dependent. Each has turned defeat into surrender and converted blind willpower into open willingness and acceptance.

Many recovering people avoid the Re-integration Stage because it, too, involves paradox. After achieving a stage of freedom and health that once seemed unattainable — and recall that they achieved it only after accepting their limitations and relinquishing the power that was not rightfully theirs — they must now *reclaim* the personal power they do possess! This is necessary work, but it is also very risky.

During this stage, chemical dependents and co-dependents weave a belief system which legitimizes self-acceptance. Self-worth stops being something that must be earned, moment by moment, through one's accomplishments or through relationship with others.

Instead, it becomes a byproduct of maintaining integrity in most areas of one's life. And how does one achieve integrity? With awareness, not denial; honesty, not secrecy; and a conscious connection with one's spiritual impulses, not arrogance. All of which can be progressively cultivated.

Entering re-integration, then, signals that one has come full circle. One has returned to being in control — but what a difference recovery makes! Control now stems from discipline rather than license.

From the outside, every recovery may look different. Individuals may enter different stages at different times, and via different routes. But those who have made great progress along this path — as measured by their internal sense of "lightness," freedom, and self-acceptance — often speak of their journeys in remarkably similar terms. The four stages outlined above represent an effort to summarize some of their wisdom.

What is important to realize for our purposes is that *there seems to be no essential difference in the recovery from chemical dependence and the recovery from co-dependence.*

Treatment for the Survival Stage (Stage I)

Treatment for the Survival Stage has three primary goals:
1. helping clients to begin dismantling their denial system;
2. helping clients to focus attention back on themselves; and
3. helping clients to begin recognizing how they are perpetuating their own problems.

A large percentage of co-dependent clients come into contact with therapists while still deeply ensconced in denial. They may have been referred by a physician. They may have sought therapy themselves for treatment of their depression, anxiety, or phobias. Or they may be cooperating with a chemical dependence treatment program, thinking that they are going to be taught how to keep their addicted family member sober. In any event, they are firmly convinced that the source of their problems lies *outside* themselves. In some cases they may not even be willing to admit that a problem exists.

Education is an important cornerstone of therapy at this point. Clients need to be exposed to information about the disease of addiction, its effects on family dynamics, the concept of co-dependence, and the process of recovery. Although this can be accomplished inside the therapy sessions or through the provision of appropriate literature, it is probably best if a series of public lectures is available to which you can make referrals. This latter approach accomplishes four goals:
- It gives clients the message that the business of recovery is not something that can be attended to only within the confines of your office or treatment center,
- It thrusts them into a setting where they will begin to receive validation for their emotions and perceptions. ("If other people feel this way, then maybe I'm not crazy.")

- It sets the stage for speaking openly about their problems.
- And, finally, it offers them the opportunity to start developing a social network of recovering friends.

Giving co-dependents simple information about themselves and about chemical dependence in general can work wonders. But what about those who become impervious to it because their denial is so strong? This is precisely the same situation that arises with chemical dependents who stay stuck in denial. And you must respond in precisely the same ways.

- *First*, you must continually comment on the existence of denial. It must be labeled as such whenever it prevents therapeutic progress.

As soon as you begin allowing bits of denial to pass without comment, you run the risk of being considered "arbitrary" if you point it out at a later time.

How can one avoid entering into a battle over denial with a client while still maintaining one's integrity as a therapist? Needless to say, this can be a delicate balancing act. It is easier to keep one's balance if it is struck from the first moment of contact with the client. The temptation to "seduce" people into therapy by failing to comment on their denial is just as problematic as "blasting" them from the outset for every iota of denial they display. For this reason, you must set the terms of the therapeutic contract from the beginning, and one of the terms must be that denial will be commented on whenever you, the treatment professional, deem it necessary in order to keep the therapy on track.

- *Second*, you must form empathic connections with your clients. Otherwise they will have no reason to tolerate having their denial commented on.

Particularly in the early stages of recovery, a client's denial will be unconscious, and anything you say about it will not make much sense to him or her. The client will perceive such comments either as personal attacks or dismiss them as the irrelevant stuff that therapists tend to go on about. He or she may listen simply because having your attention is such a novel experience.

You should approach the creation of an empathic connection with a co-dependent client in the same way you approach an unrecovering chemical dependent. Do not expect it to "take" immediately; instead, realize that your best efforts can never be anything more than invitations. An invitation can be as plain, as eloquent, as direct, or as nonthreatening as possible, but from the start you must be prepared for the fact that the client may not be interested, period. *And you must also acknowledge that you have no power to change this.* Any other attitude incorporates a co-dependent point of view that is counterproductive for all concerned.

The easiest way to form an empathic connection is by assuming that the client is in pain. The client may not be aware of his or her pain but will usually respond on some level to your communication that pain is present and that you are open to hearing about it.

Be alert to clients who claim that they do not know what they are feeling, or that they are feeling "numb." In the former case, linger on this point until the client begins to sense the frustration of being cut off from his or her emotions. Frustration is something you can empathize with, and this can be the start of the empathic connection.

When clients report that they are feeling numb, anesthetized, or simply "nothing," it is best to treat these as legitimate feelings rather than as the absence of feeling. (You might ask the client, "What does it feel like to be feeling nothing?") Co-dependents will share their feelings only with people they can trust to hear, respect, and validate them. This level of trust will not come easily, since everything they have learned up until now has taught them not to expect it. You can help by assuming that there are valid reasons behind each feeling the client is experiencing, even if those reasons are not immediately apparent.

Try to avoid being put in the position of judging whether a client's feelings are sufficiently justified by outside circumstances. Instead, simply listen, knowing that you are hearing the cries of someone who has been under an abnormal amount of stress for quite some time.

Once a client has allowed you to connect with his or her pain, two things become possible:

- You have the opportunity to model a non-co-dependent way of relating to another's feelings.

But you must be sure to feel *empathy* and not take on the client's pain as your own. This will not only frighten the client and leave him or her feeling responsible for what you are feeling; it will also lend indirect support to the co-dependent view of the world.

- You can return to that connection whenever the therapy appears to be heading into a blind alley.

In my own practice, many a co-dependent client has "proved" to me the uselessness of trusting others or of being aware of his or her feelings, only to be taken back to what I call "square one" — the fact that his or her life is filled with pain, and that something must change if that is ever going to be any different.

By continually returning to the feeling connection that has been made around the client's pain, you will be able to bring the focus back to the individual and his or her experience. Since active co-dependence involves habitually paying attention to others and their feelings, this process of making the client the primary focus represents a step in the direction of progress and health.

If there is a guiding motto for therapy at this stage, it is this: "Pain is inevitable, but misery is optional." In other words, it makes complete sense for co-dependents to feel pain and distress at what is happening to them and the people they love. It is how the client responds to that pain which determines whether it escalates into the misery of self-hatred.

Treatment for the Re-identification Stage (Stage II)

Treatment for the Re-identification Stage has four primary goals:

1. helping clients to solidify their identity as co-dependents;
2. helping clients to work through the grieving process that accompanies the loss of the illusion of power;
3. bringing clients to a new awareness of compulsivity; and
4. initiating an investigation into the realistic limits and uses of willpower.

In other words, clients need to understand that when they say they are co-dependent, they are accepting that they are powerless over areas of their lives they have long tried to control.

Education remains an important cornerstone of therapy, as it was in Stage I. Once the client's denial system has been broken, he or she is ready for assertiveness training, communication skills, and information about the multiple symptoms seen in co-dependence. The best place for such learning is in a small group setting with other co-dependents where there is ample time for discussion. (*Note:* If social skills such as assertiveness training are taught during the Survival Stage, they are likely to be used in the service of symptom abatement, which could delay entry into the Re-identification Stage.)

Working with the client's awareness of being actively co-dependent, you can begin guiding him or her through a re-interpretation of the past and the present. A tremendous amount of internalization will occur as the client stops blaming low self-esteem on outside causes and starts recognizing that it comes from having done violence to his or her own feelings, having lived a life controlled by compulsions, and having sacrificed integrity for the sake of security.

The client may experience profound depression during this stage, which you should view from its inception as an important grieving process. The relief that comes from no longer feeling responsible for the chemical dependence within the family will invariably be accompanied by a sense of loss. The client must relinquish his or her illusion of being (at least potentially) powerful enough to force the chemical dependent to become sober.

For many active co-dependents, this illusion of power is the primary source of self-esteem, and it is hard to leave behind. In fact, giving up such an important illusion is emotionally equivalent to losing a body part. It is not uncommon for clients to engage in a grieving process similar to what they might go through after the amputation of a limb.

While this is perfectly normal and even healthy, it is often profoundly confusing to clients. I point out that people only grieve over things which have truly been lost. If the client were still hanging on to the illusion of power, he or she would have no reason to grieve.

Honor the grieving and respect its intensity as a measure of how far the client has come. Meanwhile, begin helping the client to assess his or her current emotional world and come to grips with the failure of past strategies to keep life under control. Some things to explore in detail include:
- how the client went about trying to keep his or her feelings under control;
- how the client avoided acknowledging his or her personal needs; and
- how the client tried to "make" family members love him or her, feel better about themselves, and get sober.

As the client comes to an understanding of the broad range of co-dependent symptoms, your office should be a safe place for being honest about those which he or she has personally experienced. Previously buried feelings will surface; since many of these were effectively "buried alive," they may emerge with their intensity unabated. This, too, is a sign of emotional health. Unhealthy people kill their feelings before burying them. As long as feelings are still alive, they can be healed, and verbalizing them is a first step toward healing.

More than one client has said to me, "I could never let other people see me having such feelings." To which I reply, "You need the experience of having others take your feelings seriously if you're ever going to relearn how to do the same."

The Re-identification Stage is also the time to introduce the concept of compulsivity as a primary mechanism for avoiding feelings. Start by helping the client to recognize the subjective sensations associated with being in the throes of a compulsion. Once the client is able to identify these sensations for what they are, he or she can begin working toward recognizing them as they occur. And once the client has achieved this level of awareness, he or she can begin realizing that the presence of a compulsion indicates the opportunity to make a choice.

Specifically, one can choose between experiencing one's feelings — including the feelings one has previously avoided — or giving in to the compulsion. The only way to get to those previously avoided feelings is by abstaining from the compulsion.

This approach "reframes" compulsivity. The client must now decide whether to deprive himself or herself of the immediate but temporary gratification of succumbing to the compulsion, or to deprive himself or herself of feelings that will be obscured if the compulsion is allowed to take over.

This "reframing" permits only two responses, either of which has therapeutic value:

- the client may abstain from compulsions, thereby releasing emotions which have been buried for years; or
- the client may discover how difficult (and frightening) it is to abstain from something as familiar as his or her compulsions.

In other words, the client might come face-to-face with his or her own reluctance to experience feelings which have habitually been avoided. That is not a comfortable position to be in; it is never comfortable to be aware of how one resists the truth. But such awareness is a necessary precursor to change.

From a therapeutic standpoint, this discomfort can serve yet another purpose: Use it as a touchstone for creating empathy in the client for what the chemical dependent has been going through.

By focusing attention on the co-dependent's compulsivity, you are also teaching a valuable lesson about the proper role of willpower. When my clients ask what they need to do in order to defeat their compulsions, I lead them toward developing the willingness to have the feelings that will be unlocked once they become abstinent. In effect, I "reframe" the inability to abstain from compulsions as a measure of one's unwillingness to feel. Willingness, by definition, can never be forced or controlled by one's willpower. It can only be invited in — which is all that can be done with emotions one is trying to reclaim.

Treatment for the Core Issues Stage (Stage III)

Treatment for the Core Issues Stage has two primary goals:

1. helping clients to become aware of how their co-dependence has pervaded all aspects of daily life, and

2. helping clients to generalize what was learned during the Re-identification Stage about how efforts to control the chemical dependent have intensified the problem.

Until now, much of the recovery process has dealt with ending preoccupation with the chemical dependent and abstaining from compulsions (including the compulsion to control anything causing anxiety). During Stage III, co-dependents become ready for an honest self-appraisal of the ways in which they have distorted their relationships with others (not just the chemical dependent), their own emotions, and even their physical bodies through an unwillingness to accept the natural human limitations on what can and cannot be controlled. It is time for them to stop strangling life in an effort to stay "safe," and to start making friends with some of the unpredictability that real life involves.

It is during the Core Issues Stage that much of the existing therapy for co-dependence and chemical dependence becomes destructively simplistic. Several factors contribute to the deficits in the treatment available for co-dependents in this stage:

- CD family programs are limited in the number of resources they can devote to advanced recovery.

Aftercare is usually limited to still more classes (with much of the material having already been presented in other forms) and discussion groups from which old-timers gradually drop out as newcomers keep the focus on early recovery issues. Newcomers are the lifeblood of self-help meetings, but they are not necessarily what Stage III people need.

- CD therapists and treatment professionals tend to stick to highly structured counseling techniques.

While these may continue to be appropriate for some clients, they may also hold back those who are ready to deal in depth with characterological issues.

For example, many co-dependent groups begin with a meditative exercise designed to diminish anxiety, followed by a formal check-in by group members. Clients in stages I and II may require such imposed structure in order to tolerate being in groups. But some may reach the point at which they are ready to start facing the difficulty they have in letting others know their need for attention. As long as the meditation quiets their anxiety and the check-in satisfies their need for attention, they are never required to experience their usual patterns (e.g., distancing themselves from their personal needs in order to diminish their anxiety).

To rephrase an old metaphor, structured, supportive groups give people fish to eat, while interactive groups can take them through the process of learning how to catch their own fish. You give fish to people who are starving; you give the opportunity to learn how to fish to people who have regained sufficient strength and health to begin taking full responsibility for themselves.

- Co-dependents in stages I and II can be indistinguishable from borderline clients.

Often their response to therapy becomes an indispensable part of the evaluation process. Obviously some co-dependents *are* borderline and will be able to keep improving only as long as they receive treatment within a structured environment. For them, the goal of therapy should be the establishment of a strong connection to a structured setting which can then serve as a long-term resource.

However, many co-dependents who initially appear borderline will quickly appear much less so as soon as the most active phase of their disease has passed. These clients will eventually be capable of benefiting from less structured, insight-oriented therapy. Unfortunately, many therapists develop unnecessarily pessimistic prognoses for co-dependents based on the severity of their dysfunction during the active phase of their disease. A similar mistake is often made with chemical dependents when the insanity present during active alcohol and drug abuse is used to diagnose their underlying personality structure.

Treatment professionals have failed to recognize an important point: Once the dysfunction of a personality disorder is no longer present, clients with co-dependent personality *traits* can make excellent candidates for insight-oriented therapy. Motivated by the benefits they have already received from treatment, they can bring into the next level of therapy a concrete understanding of denial, an appreciation for the value of letting feelings emerge, and a realistic view of willpower — all very useful tools. Stephanie Brown has outlined a similar process by means of which recovering chemical dependents can enter very effectively into insight-ordered therapy.[2]

For the lessons learned during stages I and II to be used most effectively, however, therapists must have an intimate working knowledge of the process of recovery. While many chemical dependence therapists possess this knowledge, most therapists *outside* the CD field do not. At the same time, those *outside* the CD field tend to be the ones who are practiced in less structured, insight-oriented therapy, but few of them understand the dynamics and language of early recovery from chemical dependence and co-dependence. *What many recovering clients need is a therapist trained in both the chemical dependence and the psychodynamic traditions.*

The truth is that it is easier to find a competent CD therapist than it is to find a therapist who can do effective co-dependence treatment. CD therapists are trained to focus attention away from the past and onto the concrete behaviors required for continued sobriety. They are skilled at working with adult denial. But their training does not prepare them to deal *therapeutically* with primitive emotions intruding into an adult's life, nor are they trained in child development issues. In order to be effective as a therapist with a co-dependent in Stage III, these latter two skills are required. However, therapists from the general mental health field who possess them rarely understand the work a co-dependent client has accomplished during stages I and II. Recovering co-dependents are unlikely to form a therapeutic alliance with anyone who is unable to validate the hard-won progress they have already made.

It is during the Core Issues Stage that long-term interactive group therapy becomes valuable. The essential aspects of such groups are:
- a focus on relationships which develop and are played out among group members (attention to the "here and now");
- recognition of the problematic behavioral and emotional patterns which clients "import" into the group from their outside lives;
- encouragement of feedback by group members on how they react to each other; and
- restriction of the therapist's role to one of initially setting the group norms, paying attention to group dynamics, and facilitating recognition of behavior patterns.

The primary purpose of a long-term interactive group is to provide a setting in which the issues of co-dependence emerge *spontaneously*, rather than in response to the therapist's provocations. The relative lack of structure, combined with the presence of more people than can be monitored and controlled, will go a long way toward activating co-dependent behavior.

For the group to be truly effective, however, *the therapist must permit such behavior to emerge at its own pace.* The therapist who impatiently provokes co-dependent issues is setting himself or herself up to exercise more power than interactive group therapy can tolerate. Group members will begin interacting primarily with the therapist or with one another through the therapist. They will feel that whatever happens within the group is artificial — the result of a clever therapist's techniques.

Interactive group therapy works best when members discover themselves behaving inside the group much as they do in "real" life — being distrustful, controlling their feelings, sacrificing their own needs to ensure that others are taken care of, revealing only carefully chosen parts of themselves, covering their feelings with politeness, etc. When they finally understand that these behaviors reflect habitual and unconscious patterns, the group can become a laboratory for experimenting with alternative behaviors. The therapist's role during much of this process should be limited to promoting the feeling of safety and uncovering the reasons for any unsafe feelings group members are experiencing.

Long-term interactive, insight-oriented group therapy is extremely sophisticated work, and it is not easy to do it well. For this reason it is best for therapists to work in pairs so they can be objective for each other. *They must also be alert to the activation of co-dependent tendencies in themselves.* (Activating those tendencies is precisely what the group is supposed to do for the clients, and being a therapist does not automatically make one immune.) Even the most subtle unresolved co-dependence issues among therapists will quickly and profoundly limit the potential value of the group. Signs that these are present include:

- talking too much;
- encouraging specific feelings, such as anger;
- aborting feelings by intellectualizing or problem-solving;
- feeling clients' feelings, as opposed to feeling empathy;
- being defensive;
- being controlling;
- not tolerating silence; and
- taking action to make the group "work" (for example, be interesting and sufficiently emotional) rather than exploring why it is stuck.

Finally, it is important to recognize that interactive group therapy is a very delicate flower that must be painstakingly cultivated. Whenever therapists mix experiential work, individual work, education, and supportive techniques into an interactive group, the essence of interactional therapy is quickly diluted and lost. It does little good to "trust the process" only halfway, since half-hearted efforts give mixed messages about how much responsibility the therapist is willing to place on the clients. *Co-dependents in Stage III are ready to accept full responsibility for their own therapy.*

Treatment for the Re-integration Stage (Stage IV)

Therapy during the Re-integration Stage has one primary goal: preparing clients for termination.

The line between stages III and IV is both fine and ephemeral. Clients may spend considerable time moving back and forth across it. On occasion they may even work with one foot planted firmly on each side. It is during the process of termination that most clients first experiment with planting both feet in the new territory of Stage IV. If they are truly ready to terminate, their autonomy will be firmly established, self-esteem will be legitimized by an integrated belief system, and serenity will be experienced on occasion.

Much of the therapy suggested for stages I through III is geared toward helping clients reach this stage. All too often, overly simplistic treatment for co-dependents tries to teach self-esteem, relaxation, and serenity through didactic classes, role-playing, and endless repetition of the Serenity Prayer. Lectures on assertiveness and building positive self-worth are offered during the first four weeks of most family treatment programs. For co-dependents in early recovery, these classes can be refreshing and useful for instilling hope and a blush of self-confidence.

However, an active co-dependent's character structure is impervious to fully internalizing lessons about self-esteem. Being good "co's," clients are capable of learning such lessons rapidly, understanding them intellectually, and giving the appearance of having incorporated them into their lives. Once we accept that co-dependence is a recognizable Mixed Personality Disorder, it becomes clear that short-term methods can effect only superficial changes.

The characterological changes necessary for co-dependents to internalize a new belief system legitimizing self-acceptance usually begin during the Core Issues Stage. At this point many clients have the urge to terminate therapy — a sign that co-dependence is still active. This urge stems from an old strategy of grasping tightly to any feelings of relief and self-worth. Continued treatment is seen as a threat rather than a support for any progress which has already been made.

Many therapists feel tempted to validate *too* quickly the client's newfound sense of independence by refraining from a full exploration of what termination means. Clients who are pushed to explore their feelings about termination may well exhibit normal defensive reactions, such as accusing the therapist of trying to foster dependence or of not having enough faith in their ability to stay healthy. Use this as a rule of thumb: When clients are *really* ready to terminate, they will recognize these defenses as a way of resisting experiencing the emotions associated with termination — and they will be willing to become conscious of these feelings.

When clients do choose to terminate abruptly out of fear that further work in therapy will challenge their newfound sense of independence and power, or because they are not willing to explore their feelings during the act of separation, do not dwell on this choice as a failure. Instead, review the progress the client has made so far and end with an open invitation to reenter therapy at any time. If appropriate, you may predict the probability that specific events in the client's future life may well activate additional issues. Note that the client has learned to understand the meaning of his or her feelings and to discover alternative ways of dealing with these events.

One of the last skills therapists fully develop is that of approaching termination as both an integral part of successful therapy and an opportunity to deal with several important issues which may have been avoided until then. In other words, termination becomes a process, not an event, which the therapist has woven throughout the treatment. Part of this process involves facilitating the client's growth from dependence on the therapist to being autonomous. In most cases this dependence began as an unhealthy, co-dependent craving for validation, then gradually grew into a relationship of trust in an atmosphere of safety that the client relied on to incubate his or her early efforts at independence. As in any relationship designed to help a person evolve into an autonomous, self-reliant individual, there comes a time when the dependence must come to an end. This is a time of mixed sadness and joy. When a client is capable of experiencing and tolerating this complex blend of emotions, he or she is probably ready to begin thinking seriously about terminating therapy. Naturally, it is best for the client's growth if the therapist is also ready to let go.

For some clients, termination represents the first time in their lives that they will voluntarily leave a relationship. They may feel a sense of guilt for abandoning someone (the therapist) who respected them even before they respected themselves. They may feel anxious about being on their own. They may frighten themselves by the degree to which they regress once termination becomes a realistic prospect. Working through the process of termination gives ancient issues of abandonment and separation enough time to surface. On occasion, these issues can be so significant that the therapy enters a deeper level of work.

Successful termination can be an event of rare beauty. Being with a client who keeps his or her eyes open while saying "goodbye" is quite moving. To experience the *act of separating* as opposed to one's *fears of separation* is to stay in relationship during one of the most difficult moments any relationship can encompass. The decision to stay aware of one's feelings no matter what is happening is the essence of recovery. If you are met with such behavior in a client, take it as cause for joy.

The Co-Dependent Professional

It is possible, of course, for therapists to exhibit co-dependent characteristics. It is even more likely if they come from chemically dependent homes or backgrounds — as a disproportionate percentage do. (This has prompted one leader in the field to term counselors one of the "byproducts" of chemically dependent families.) If you have spent your life practicing staying sane in the midst of insanity, going into the mental health field makes a lot of sense!

It also makes sense that children from chemically dependent families would grow up knowing the devastation that chemical dependence can cause. They have no trouble taking it seriously. Unfortunately, becoming a mental health or CD professional puts them at great risk of having any unresolved co-dependent tendencies activated. Like Daniel walking back into the lion's den, they come into contact on a daily basis with clients who exhibit the denial, projection, and rationalization that were typical in the homes they grew up in.

An especially prevalent form of denial among professionals who are recovering from their own co-dependence stems from a minimization of how much personal recovery is necessary before one can start treating others. On the one hand, recovering chemical dependents are routinely cautioned against prematurely becoming CD therapists. On the other, many therapists rush into treating co-dependent clients soon after they discover their own issues with co-dependence. This is particularly common among therapists who are adult children of alcoholics. A moment's reflection should reveal that any minimization of the time and effort needed to recover from Co-Dependent Personality

Disorder is *de facto* evidence that co-dependent denial is still active. *If therapists hope to help clients understand co-dependence as the serious dysfunction it is, then those recovering from their own co-dependence must be willing to take steps to heal themselves first.* Whether this occurs in a Twelve Step program, in therapy, or both, it will take substantial time and dedication — often as long as two years or more.

A second factor leading to active co-dependence among professionals is the very nature of their job. Almost by definition, therapists are expected to keep their personal needs on the back burner while they work to be present for their clients. The whole focus of the therapeutic relationship is the growth of the client, and therapists are expected to have that as their guiding principle. They are taught to maintain a sense of control throughout any therapeutic session. It is up to them to create a safe environment for the client. They are expected to be able to tolerate any intensity of feeling in the room in order to model that there is nothing to fear from experiencing emotions. They learn not to react defensively to the taunts, slights, and occasional scorn that clients send their way. With all these messages about what a good therapist should be able to do, no wonder the job is a set-up for activating — and rewarding — co-dependent tendencies!

When a therapist's own co-dependence becomes active, he or she displays the same symptoms of *pride*, *shame*, and *doubt* seen in unrecovering clients. A therapist may take excessive pride in the power of therapy and start believing that therapists are capable of controlling all manner of things. Rescue fantasies abound. Professional pomposity creeps in, and the therapist starts believing that he or she is capable of manipulating clients into being healthy. This overblown sense of the power of therapy is a sign that the will is running rampant.

Pride can also lead therapists to take excessive credit for the progress their clients make. This is not only patronizing to clients but also eventually adds an extra burden to the therapeutic relationship which is destructive to a good treatment alliance. It gives clients power over the therapist's self-esteem which they will sense on at least an unconscious level, and it makes the therapist vulnerable to a loss of self-worth when the client fails to make progress or needs to regress in the service of his or her therapy.

When therapists feel shame, it is usually because they have fallen into the co-dependent trap of feeling inadequate. They are convinced that they can "make" their clients improve; when this doesn't happen, they blame themselves. Their sense of well-being becomes attached to how well (or inappropriately) the client behaves, which is very reminiscent of the co-dependent's relationship with the chemical dependent.

We can appreciate the delicacy of the therapist's position. Naturally therapists want their clients to show improvement and dislike seeing them founder. But when therapists react to their clients' progress (or lack thereof) with more than pleasure or displeasure, the presence of professional co-dependence is revealed. When therapists invest their own self-esteem in clients' performance, and thus become proud or shamed by another's behavior, they have begun to model co-dependence themselves.

Similarly, when a therapist loses sight of the distinction between his or her personal identity and role as a professional, he or she displays the co-dependent symptom of doubt. In their pursuit of authenticity, many therapists strive to obliterate the distinction between themselves as people and themselves as therapists. In fact, many therapists arrive at the conclusion that being as personally authentic and natural as possible is the *essence* of doing therapy. Not so! The therapist who strives only for authenticity is like the athlete who works only to stay in good physical shape. There is far more to being an athlete than that — such as mastering the rules of the game, practicing the appropriate skills, and understanding the underlying strategies. As much as therapists might wish that personal health, openness, and confidence were all it took to help their clients, these are only the *basics* necessary to do a good job.

Every therapeutic relationship is actually a triad involving the client, the *person* who is acting as therapist, and the *role* of the therapist. The role itself has an element of autonomy which sometimes demands that the person playing it give specific responses to a client, regardless of what he or she may feel like doing. In addition, the role is licensed and should be open to public scrutiny. This means that while the therapist's personal life may be reserved from the public eye, anything he or she does in the role of a therapist is ultimately a matter of public record and subject to public comment.

Therapeutic authenticity exists when therapists can allow the role to possess its required autonomy, without doing any violence to who they are personally. When the professional falls into doubt about the boundaries which must be maintained between the role of therapist and his or her personal needs, the role begins to lose its autonomy. It starts to shift and sway under the pressure of client demands. The therapist's personal needs to feel warm and giving may intrude on what good therapeutic practice stipulates should be done for the client's sake at that point. Or the therapist's need to be seen as an authority may take precedence over other more appropriate considerations.

What it boils down to is this: Therapists are more effective when they are not personally overidentified with their role. When they are in doubt about who they are *vs.* what they do, this might appropriately be suspected as a sign of professional co-dependence.

For *every* client in *every* situation, the therapist must continually assess what is therapeutic and what is not. Once a particular action has been deemed therapeutic, it is a sign of co-dependence if the therapist talks himself or herself out of taking that action in order to avoid dealing with the client's reaction. Every therapist has struck such a bargain with better judgment at one time or another, but when it becomes *habitual* it may indicate that personal co-dependence issues are being played out in the therapist-client relationship. In this case the therapist should seek help.

When consultation is not sought at such times, it is best to recall that the avoidance of outside support is one of the hallmarks of co-dependence.

---

[1]The stages of recovery model presented here relies heavily on work done by Stephanie Brown, Herbert Gravitz, and Julie Bowden.
See Stephanie Brown, Ph.D., *Treating the Alcoholic* (New York: John Wiley & Sons, 1985) and Herbert Gravitz, Ph.D., and Julie Bowden, M.F.C.C., *Guide to Recovery* (Holmes Beach, Florida: Learning Publications, 1985).
[2]Stephanie Brown, ibid.

PART FOUR

THE FUTURE OF CO-DEPENDENCE

The concept of co-dependence is in its very earliest stages of development. Several problems remain to be solved if it is going to gain further acceptance and be developed into a sophisticated tool for helping professionals.
- First, there is not yet sufficient data for co-dependence to be proposed for inclusion in the next revision of DSM.

The diagnostic criteria recommended here are intended to provide a substantive framework for thinking about co-dependence. I hope that these criteria will stimulate some of the research required to establish scientific validity and reliability for viewing co-dependence as a legitimate personality disorder. Until sufficient empirical studies have been completed, it is premature to expect co-dependence to formally be included in the DSM nomenclature.

The process of pathologizing human behavior is dangerous and should be entered into only under the weight of compelling evidence. In the case of co-dependence, however, I believe that we can say with assurance that it *acts* like a disease, with discernible symptoms which are predictable, progressive, and debilitating. Furthermore, the value to clients of taking on the label of co-dependence is indisputable. It is certainly appropriate at this point to begin a more rigorous process of collecting data about co-dependence.

- Second, the characteristics of co-dependence outlined herein obviously have wider application than to the CD field alone.

Children from non-chemically dependent homes that harbor chronic disabilities, secrets, and cruelties also demonstrate the symptoms of PTSD and co-dependence later in life. Spouses who have been physically abused often show active co-dependence even when chemical dependence is not present.

Exactly what are the conditions which combine to produce co-dependence? Living in a committed relationship with a chemical dependent apparently contains a concentrated dose of many of the critical features in the etiology of this disease. But much more research needs to be done to ascertain other, broader parameters capable of producing it.

- Third, it is possible that allowing co-dependence into our diagnostic nomenclature would open a Pandora's box.

Even if a stable and predictable pattern of personality traits results from living in a committed relationship with a chemical dependent, and these traits can rigidify or intensify to the point of creating sufficient dysfunction to fall under the rubric of Mixed Personality Disorder, would there be problems involved in formally including co-dependence in DSM? Would every mental health special-interest group that can define a syndrome with statistical significance demand similar formal recognition?

Would there be professional lobbyists for Post-Divorce Personality Disorder, Step-Family Disorder, etc., *ad infinitum*?

I don't know the answers, but neither do I believe that admitting co-dependence into the accepted diagnostic nomenclature would start a stampede. Any problems regarding how the mental health profession does and doesn't recognize and label illnesses are problems that already exist.

This book poses a *single* question: whether co-dependence meets the same standards for a personality disorder that *already* apply to the current categories.

- Fourth, the speed of improvement seen in some recovering co-dependents argues against conceptualizing their condition as a character disorder.

Character disorders are often considered difficult to treat successfully. But some co-dependents experience quick improvement with a primarily educational and supportive approach. It is absurd to think that a borderline or a narcissistic personality disorder could experience similar progress during (or immediately after) a four-week series of lectures. Does this mean that we are exaggerating the seriousness of co-dependence?

Two responses to this final objection come to mind. First, it might not be as absurd as it seems to consider giving concentrated doses of direct education to a wider variety of clients. And second, the disease of co-dependence, like the disease of chemical dependence, is truly a disease of denial — much more so than the traditional personality disorders.

Once a client's denial system has started to crumble, there is a critical period of vulnerability during which education is most effective. After this initial period passes, it frequently becomes less valuable to expose the client to educational modalities. In any illness, the time immediately after a bit of denial is relinquished is one during which new input is most likely to be accepted. In the case of co-dependence, the amount of denial relinquished is often massive, thereby allowing the educational approach to be temporarily extremely powerful.

Co-dependence is a definable entity which has been discovered and conceptualized within the CD field. This turns the tables on the rest of the mental health field; traditionally, CD professionals have learned from *them* and imported *their* latest theories into the CD field, not the other way around. In this instance, however, the CD field has a contribution to make to the wider mental health field.

I believe that the future will see the exportation of co-dependence into the general mental health field as a didactic tool, a psychological concept, and eventually a diagnostic category. When that happens, one remaining problem may be solved: its name.

Few people are satisfied with the term "co-dependence," and efforts to find a better one have met with a creative vacuum.

Finally, I believe that definitions of co-dependence have failed to coalesce because we have been trying to simplify the concept, and this is ultimately the wrong approach. Co-dependence actually falls into a class of psychological concepts that are distinguished by even greater complexity than most. This complexity arises from the fact that co-dependence simultaneously refers both to *intrapsychic* and to *interpersonal* dynamics. It is this complexity that raises it above simply being a rediscovery or restatement of personality disorders.

Our language in psychology generally divides into two realms. Terms referring to intrapsychic phenomena (e.g. ego, unconscious, anxiety, defenses, etc.) occupy one realm, while terms referring to interpersonal interactions (e.g. enmeshment, family systems, role reversal, etc.) occupy another. Relatively few terms apply to both. One notable exception, and perhaps the prototype for such a multilevel concept, is *projective identification*, a term introduced by Melanie Klein in 1946.[1]

An example of projective identification would be the following: A man discovers that his car has been stolen. His fear of anger (to which he gave destructive license during his active chemical dependence) causes him to immediately repress this feeling. Although his tone of voice and demeanor reveal the unconscious anger, he is only aware of feeling vulnerable and sad. The man further defends against his anger by projecting it out into the environment — specifically, onto his wife. She in turn gets uncharacteristically angry at the insurance adjuster for taking too long to respond. The man then runs to the adjuster's defense.

An analysis of these interactions, in order to be complete, must take into account how the intrapsychic and interpersonal interactions are intertwined. The man projected his anger outward. The wife identified with it. And the man was left with "evidence" that the anger really *did* originate outside himself — hence his defense of the insurance adjuster.

In projective identification, one person's projections are absorbed and confirmed by another person's behavior. It is a single, unifying concept that refers, in its pathologic extreme, to the complementary roles two Personality Disordered individuals can play for each other. Co-dependence likewise refers not only to an identifiable Personality Disorder (Echo), but also to its characteristically dysfunctional style of interacting with specific other Personality Disorders (Narcissus).

Once the true complexity of co-dependence is acknowledged, it becomes apparent why the definitions frequently seem to compete with one another. Each definition tends to focus more on either the intrapsychic or the interpersonal realm, while co-dependence itself exists on both levels. Closer study of how projective identification links these two levels may guide us toward developing a better understanding of co-dependence, while humbling those who are intent on simple explanations.

Co-dependence will one day be better characterized as a disease of relationships. Whether those relationships are between self and feelings or self and others, the problems are the same. The current nomenclature for describing distortions in relationships that span intrapsychic and interpersonal realms is meager at best. Even our ability to conceptualize on such a complex plane is poorly developed. Yet it is in this direction that the concept of co-dependence points.

---

[1]See Leonard Horowitz, "Projective Identification in Dyads and Groups," *International Journal of Group Psychotherapy* 33 (1983), pp. 259-279.

AFTERWORD

Lost in the theoretical threads which have been woven back and forth have been the countless number of individual stories unfolding in the moment. Millions of lives are currently being lived in isolation and quiet desperation. Whatever we choose as a term to refer to these individuals, it will never be able to convey the reality of their hopelessness, their pain, and their fear.

This work is dedicated to all those who have suffered as a result of the disease of chemical dependence, whether from its direct effects or from the co-dependence which almost inevitably surrounds it. By speaking openly about the family aspects of this disease, perhaps we can find a way to give Echo back her own voice.

INDEX

Abandonment, felt during therapy
 termination   92-93
Abstinence
   compulsive behavior and   28
   pain of   70
Acceptance of a label   71-72
Acceptance of limitations   72-73
Adaptation to Life   20
Addiction defined   6
Addictive process defined   6
Addictive thinking   74
Adult children of abusers
   of alcoholics   54-55
   PTSD therapy   65
   as therapists   93
Adult Children of Alcoholics
 group   67
Adult emotions   87
Aftercare   62, 67-68, 85
Al-Anon   34, 62, 67-68
   meetings for co-dependents   45-46
Alateen   62
Alcohol Dependence, self-esteem
 and   12
Alcoholic thinking   30, 74
Alcoholics Anonymous   67-68
Alexander, Charles   2
Anxiety
   change and   63
   hypervigilance and   57
   intimacy and separation   18-20
   as symptom of co-dependence
    28-29
Apathetic co-dependents   39-40
Assertiveness training   81
Authenticity in therapy   95-96
Autonomy   52
   in re-integration stage   91-92
   therapist's role   96
Axis A (willpower)   51
Axis B (personal needs)   51-52
Axis C (autonomy)   52

Behavioral co-dependence   5-6
Birth defects   54
Black, Claudia   4
Blackouts, violence during   31-33
Bonding   xi
Borderline Personalities   59
Borderline Personality Disorder
   core issues treatment   86-89
   interpersonal distance   19-20
Boundary distortions of intimacy
 and separation   18-20
Bowden, Julie   97
Brown, Stephanie   87, 97

Caretaker role   5
Catharsis therapy   64
Characterological change,
 re-integration and   91-92
Chemical dependence   4

Chemical dependence (continued)
  current use 63
  physical and sexual abuse during 32-33
  as symptom of co-dependence 29-31
Child development issues 87
Children
  of alcoholics 54-55
  emotional deprivation and 26
  physical and sexual abuse 32-33
  PTSD therapy 65
  who become counselors 93-94
Client-person-role triad 96
Co-alcoholic 4
Co-conspirators 37-38
Co-dependence
  accepting label 72
  clinical examples 40-50
  conditions for 100
  criteria 3
  defined 1-7
  diagnostic criteria 10-59
  didactic tool 2
  disease entity 3
  failure of definitions 102-104
  future trends 99-104
  global definition 6
  levels of meaning 1-2
  origins of word 4
  as personality disorder 100-101
  psychological concept 2-3
  research on vii-viii
  residential treatment 64
  social context 9
  symptoms 20-35
  theoretical frameworks 1-2
  in therapists 89, 93-97
  therapy overview 61-63
  as transmitter for chemical dependence 50
  variants of 36-40
Co-Dependent Personality Disorder 10, 93-94

diagnostic criteria 11-36
duality with Borderline Personality Disorder 20
Co-dependent thinking (co-ing) 30
Co-ing 30
  vs. helping 50-53
Communication skills 81
Compulsive behavior 27-28
  re-identification therapy 83-84
Confusion of identities 13-14
Constriction of emotions 23-25
  in family therapy 43-44
Core issues stage of recovery 74-75
  treatment 84-90
Cork, Margaret 54
Counselors as byproducts of dependence 93-94
Counterphobic behavior 18
Crisis as recovery tool 71
Criterion A (self-esteem) 12-16, 42
  in family therapy 44
  in stress-related illness 45
Criterion B (responsibility) 17-18, 42
  in stress-related illness 45
Criterion C (anxiety and intimacy) 18-20, 42
  in family therapy 44
  stress-related illness 45
Criterion D (relationships) 20-21
  stress-related illness 45
Criterion E (behavioral symptoms) 21-35, 42
  hypervigilance 57
  psychic numbing 56
  in stress-related illness 45

Death instinct 6
Defense mechanisms 20-21
Denial
  among therapists 93-94
  as disease 101-102
  excessive reliance on 22-23
  in co-dependents 14-15, 69-70
  in family therapy 42-44

Denial (continued)
    of limitations 70
    by observers 45-46
    in re-identification stage 70-71
    in survival stage 69-70
    treatment for in survival stage 77-81
Dependent Personality Disorder 13
    assuming responsibility 17-18
    self-esteem and 12
Depersonalization 24
Depression 58
    admitting 25-26
    during re-identification stage 82
Deprivation 26
Detoxification process 63-64
Diagnostic nomenclature,
 co-dependence in 100-101
Disease
    co-dependence as 100
    defined 35-36
Dissociation 24
Doubt 53
    in co-dependent therapists 94-95
Drinking partner 38-39
Drug mentality 30
Drugging partner 38-39
Dry chemical dependents 72-74
DSM III (*Diagnostic and Statistical Manual*, Third Edition) 1, 7
    co-dependence included in 99-100
    personality traits and disorders 9
Dysfunction and personality
 disorder 10

Eating disorders 54
Echo ix-xii, 103, 105
Education
    in re-identification stage
     therapy 81-82
    in survival stage therapy 77
    as therapeutic tool 101-102
Ego psychology 5
Emotional control 64-65

Emotional outbursts 24-25
Emotions, constriction of 23-25
Empathic connection in client-
 therapist 78-80
Enabling behavior 37-38
Enmeshment in relationships 20-21
Existential dread 28-29

False self 29
Family disease, co-dependence
 as viii
Family education program 62
Family systems defined 4-5
Family therapy
    early recovery 42-44
    vs. co-dependent therapy 62
Fetal alcohol syndrome 54
Financial resources for recovery 85
Forgotten Children, The 54
Foster care 54
Freud, Sigmund
    on death instinct 6
    on narcissism xi-xii
Friel, John 5
Friel, Linda 5
Frustration as therapeutic tool 79

Gestalt therapy 66
Gravitz, Herbert 97
Greenleaf, Jael 58
Grieving process 82
Group therapy
    interactive 88
    vs. individual therapy 65-66
Guilt of survivor 57-58

Home environment 63-64
Horowitz, Leonard 104
Hyperactivity 54
Hypervigilance 26-27, 57

Identity confusion 13-14
I'll Quit Tomorrow 30

Individual therapy 41-42
  vs. group therapy 65-66
Insight-oriented therapy 87-88
Integrity, recovery and 76
Inter-dependence 13
Interactive counseling
  techniques 85-88
Internalization 81-82
Interpersonal dynamics 102-103
Intervention 71
Intimacy and boundary
  distortions 18-20
Intrapsychic dynamics 102-103
"Ism" of Alcoholism 30, 68, 72-74
Isolation of co-dependents 12

Johnson, Vernon 30
  "ism" of alcoholism 68

Klein, Melanie 3, 103

Larsen, Earnie 5

Managing fallacy 24
Martyr behavior in
  co-dependents 5, 34-37
Meditative exercise 85-86
Metamorphoses ix-xi
Mixed Personality Disorder 1-2,
  10, 100

Narcissism x-xii
Narcissistic Personality
  Disorder 10
Narcissus ix-xii, 103
Negative feelings, constriction
  of 23
Nonpsychotic Psychological
  Disorders 35
Norwood, Robin 5
Numbness 24
  legitimacy of 79-80
  psychic 56

Overpersonalization 20-21
Ovid ix-xi

Pain
  awareness of, in therapy 79-81
  as weapon against denial 69-71
Passivity 34-35
People-pleaser role 5
Perfectionist behavior 5
Persecutors, co-dependents as 37
Personal needs 51-52
Personality disorders 9, 108
  see also Borderline, Co-dependent,
    Dependent, Mixed, Narcissistic
    Personality Disorders
Personality traits 9
Physical abuse 31-33
  of children 54
Post-Traumatic Stress Disorder
  (PTSD) 3, 26-27
  in children 55-56
  therapy 64-65
Power, illusion of 82
Power of therapy 94
Preferences 17
Pride 53
  in co-dependent therapists 94-95
Projective identification 3, 103-104
Psychic numbing 24, 56, 79-80
Psychodrama 66
Psychodynamic therapy 87
Psychotic denial 22
  see also Denial
Public lectures 77

Re-experiencing trauma 55-56
Re-identification stage 70-74
  treatment for 81-84
Re-integration stage 75-76
  treatment 90-93
Recovery
  chemical dependents vs.
    co-dependents 75-76

INDEX

Recovery (continued)
  core issues stage 74-75
  process of 66-67
  re-identification stage 70-74
  re-integration stage 75-76
  stages of 68-76
  survival stage 69-70
Reframing compulsivity 83-84
Rejection by client, dealing with 78-79
Relationships, co-dependence as disease of 104
Rescue fantasies 94
Residential treatment 63-64
Responsibility, assuming 17-18
Runaways 54

Sacrifice xi-xii
  autonomy and 52
  see also Martyr behavior
Schaef, Anne Wilson 6
School problems and co-dependence 54
Security, denial as 22-23
Self-acceptance 75-76
Self-esteem
  acceptance of 75-76
  in children of dependents 54-55
  co-dependence and 12-16
  dependence on others for 15-16
  during re-identification therapy 82
  in therapists 95
Separation
  anxiety and boundary distortions 18-20
  from therapy 92-93
Serenity Prayer 90
Sexual abuse 31-33
  children 54
Shame 53
  in co-dependent therapists 94-95
Spirituality in therapy 68
Stinking thinking 30

Stress
  numbing 56
  physical signs of 33-34
Stress-related medical illness 33-34
  failure of therapy 44-46
  as sign of co-dependence 44-46
Structured counseling techniques 85-86
  inadequacy in re-integration stage 90-91
Stuttering 54
Subby, Robert 5
Substance abuse as symptom 29-31
Suicide in co-dependents 39-40
Survival stage of recovery 69-70
  treatment for 77-81
Survivor guilt 57-58
Symptom therapy for co-dependents 61-62

Tap Dancer role 5
Teenage pregnancy and prostitution 54
Termination of therapy 91-92
Theoretical framework for co-dependency 3-7
Therapeutic contract 78
Transgenerational diagrams 46-50
Twelve Step Program 62, 67-68
  re-identification stage 72-73
Two-year time limit 34-35

Unrecovering family members 41-42

Vaillant, George 20
Verbalization of feelings 83
Violence and co-dependence 31-33

Wegscheider-Cruse, Sharon 6
  transgenerational diagrams 49
Whitfield, Charles 5
Willingness
  vs. willfulness 12
  willpower and 84

Willpower
  co-dependence and 12
  co-ing vs. helping 51
  compulsive behavior and 84
  confusion of identities
    and 13-14
  in core issues stage 74-75
  limitations 72-73
Winning through losing
 paradox 74-75
Withdrawal symptoms 69
Workaholic role 5

Zen of willpower 75

Need a copy for a friend?
You may order directly.

DIAGNOSING AND TREATING CO-DEPENDENCE:
A guide for professionals who work with chemical dependents,
their spouses and children

by Timmen L. Cermak, M.D.
Chairman, National Association for Children of Alcoholics

$8.95

Order Form

Please send _____ copy (copies) of DIAGNOSING AND TREATING CO-DEPENDENCE by Timmen L. Cermak, M.D.

Price $8.95 per copy. Please add $1.00 shipping for the first book and 25¢ for each additional copy.

_____
Name (please print)

_____
Address

_____
City/State/Zip

_____ (   ) _____
Attention   *Telephone*

Please note that orders under $15.00 must be pre-paid.

If paying by credit card, please complete the following:

☐ Bill the full payment to my credit card.
☐ VISA ☐ MasterCard ☐ American Express

Credit card number: _____

For faster service, call our
Order Department TOLL-FREE:
1-800-231-5165

In Minnesota call:
1-800-247-0484

For MASTERCARD:
Write the 4 digits below the account number: _____

Expiration date: _____ Signature on card: _____

Return this order form to: The Johnson Institute
                             510 First Avenue North
                             Minneapolis, MN 55403-1607

Ship to (if different from above):

Name _____

Address _____

City/State/Zip _____